Mysteries and Secrets Revealed! ③

W9-BIT-769

The Unofficial Guide

Not authorized by GAINAX/ProjectEva. or TV TOKYO

cocoro books

Published by DH Publishing, Inc.
2-3-3F Kanda Jimbocho, Chiyoda-ku
Tokyo 101-0051, Japan
www.dhp-online.com

cocoro books is an imprint of DH Publishing, Inc.

First published 2004

Text and illustrations c 2004 by DH Publishing, Inc.

Printed in USA

Printed by Delta Printing Solutions, Inc.
Compiled by Kazuhisa Fujie and Martin Foster
Publisher: Hiroshi Yokoi
Publications Director: Clive Victor France
Design: Kyoichi Akimoto
Editor: Takako Aoyama

ISBN 0-9745961-4-0

All Rights Reserved. No part of this publication may be reproduced,
stored in a retrieval system, or transmitted in any form or by any means,
electronic, mechanical, photocopying, recording,
or otherwise without the written consent of the publisher.

THIS BOOK IS NOT AFFILLIATED WITH OR ENDORSED BY
GAINAX/ProjectEva. or TV TOKYO

Neon Genesis Evangelion
The Unofficial Guide

How to Use

In this book, the third in the popular Mysteries and Secrets Revealed! anime series, you'll find everything you need to know about Neon Genesis Evangelion and much more! And it's so easy to use! Just follow the simple EVA code below and within a few hours you'll be an Evangelion expert.

Questions and Answers

Want to find out why who did what when and where? Then this is the book for you. 45 questions and detailed answers on every Evangelion topic, from characters and relationships to Evangelions and Angels.

Glossary

When you speak the lingo everything is so much easier. At the back of this book you'll find a glossary stuffed full of names, what they mean and which pages to find them on.

Keyword Index

Want to go straight to New Tokyo-3? Then start at the alphabetical Keyword Index at the back of the book. There you'll find page links to every destination in the Evangelion world.

EVA Files + Profiles

Scattered throughout the book are 6 EVA Files and 14 EVA Profiles that introduce you to an altogether different side of Evangelion and the characters that have made it so popular. Check out Eva figures and merchandise, Eva cosplay, Eva events, movies, the industry and Eva history. Profiles on all the leading characters, including Shinji, Rei, Asuka, Kaoru, Misato and many more!

Neon Genesis Evangelion: The Core

EVA Profiles

EVA Files

The Secret of Evangelion's Success

One of the driving forces behind Evangelion's popularity in Japan is the use of many girl characters that appeal to stay-at-home *otaku*: girls with minds of their own; ill-fated young women; intellectual types; and dependable big-sister types.

The fact that the supporting female roles diverted popularity away from the lead character Shinji and the featured mechanical innovation – the Evas – is proof that Evangelion is different from other anime series of the period. It is no surprise to learn that figures and other merchandise of the supporting female characters outsold everything else.

Evangelion is perhaps the most extraordinary robot animation series ever made. Apart from having a complicated plot, the creator purposely leaves many mysteries – especially those related to the characters themselves – unexplained until the final episode.

The Three Major Elements of Evangelion's Success

It is said that *Gundam* changed the basic storyline of robot anime by moving away from simple good and evil, placing the emphasis on the conflicts between human beings.

That clearly differentiates it from other animated robot series, such as *Mazinga Z* where there was an easy-to-follow storyline involving evil robots and the protectors of justice who fought them.

Evangelion manages to focus the viewer's interest on the complicated elements of the story, leaving a plethora of mysteries remaining, such as - Why were the Evas created? Why do the Evas fight? Just who are the Evas' opponents - the Angels? All of these mysteries draw the viewer back to the next episode.

In addition, the underlying theme of Christianity in Evangelion gives it religious, philosophical and psychological overtones that have made it popular with older viewers.

The Appeal of the Characters

The average introspective junior high school kid is able to associate with Evangelion, as it shifts the emphasis of the robot story from brave, shining examples of justice fighting for the rights of the planet to a weak, shy junior high school kid who has no interest in fighting.

The creators surround this lead character with a bunch of girls who would also appeal to less extroverted types.

Furthermore, all the characters have extremely complicated inner-worlds, and the descriptions of what is going on in each character's mind are also elements that set Evangelion apart from other anime series. Having said which, the deliberate omission of explanations is equally important, especially when it relates to the actions of the characters.

In many cases, these go unexplained, leaving the viewer to substitute supposition and analysis for fact, which lends an almost literary element to the story. With Evangelion, fans focus more on the characters than the mechanics.

The Power of Imitation

Evangelion carries a large number of quotes from and references to other anime productions, such as *Ultraman, Space Battleship Yamato* and *Gundam.* The works of Go Nagai – such as *Mazinga Z* – and even the novelist Ryu Murakami are also referred to. This was so apparent that Evangelion became known as the "remixed anime."

For example, the camera angle in one of the Eva fighting scenes is taken directly from *Ultraman,* while some of the names of the characters are lifted from the Murakami novel *Ai to Genso no Fascism (Fascism in Love and Fantasy*). This has been a boon to anime die-hards intent on tracking every influence.

Overview

The animated series *Neon Genesis Evangelion* 2 – produced by Gainax, and directed by Hideaki Anno – was broadcast on Japanese TV for approximately six months from October 1995, but the story came to no conclusive end even with the *Final Episode.* We all had to wait until *The End of Evangelion* released in the summer of 1997 to see the de facto end to the story.

The End of Evangelion was a remake of the *Second Final Episode* (Episode 25 and the final episode) made for TV, which came in the wake of the movie *Death and Rebirth* released in spring 1997, a recollection of the TV series along with previews of a film covering the complete story.

The DVD and video of *The End of Evangelion (Air/My Pure Heart for You*) in circulation at present – released by Gainax – has been recorded with "slight modifications" following Episode 25th for TV and *Final Episode.*

The movie *Death and Rebirth* was released between the end of the TV series and before the release of *The End of Evangelion*, and in terms of content is positioned as a digest of the TV series - *Death* - and a preview of the completed work – *Rebirth*.

Rebirth is the first half of the *Air* portion of *The End of Evangelion*. As a result, when we watch *The End of Evangelion* we can see that it also includes *Rebirth*. In other words, they overlap. So, *Death and Rebirth* can be passed over without leaving any loose ends as far as gaining an understanding of the overall story.

Neon Genesis Evangelion 2 for TV: No real end despite having a final episode.
The movies *Death and Rebirth*: *Death* is a remake of the TV series and *Rebirth* is a preview of *The End of Evangelion*.
The movie *The End of Evangelion*: A continuation of Episode 24 shown on TV, with *Air* as Episode 25 and *Magokoro wo Kimi ni* as Episode 26.

Chronology

Mar. 30, 1977	Birth of Yui Ikari
1999	Gendo Ikari, Kozo Fuyutsuki and Yui meet up for the first time
Sept. 12, 2000	Gendo returns to Japan from the South Pole
Sept. 13, 2000	The occurrence of the Second Impact at the South Pole. Two billion human lives are lost as a result. (The official explanation is that a meteorite hit the pole. The meteorite is relatively small – not even 10 cm in circumference, but was traveling at 95% the speed of light when it hit the earth. It is also reported that the meteor was spotted 15 minutes before impact by Seymore Nan, an amateur astronomist in Mexico.) Birth of Kaoru Nagisa
Sept. 15, 2000	Refugees clash on the Indo-Pakistan border, which escalates into a military conflict.
Sept. 20, 2000	New-type bomb – believed to be an N2 bomb – dropped on Tokyo, killing 500,000 people.
Feb. 14, 2001	Valentine's Treaty/Special Ceasefire
June 6, 2001	Birth of Shinji Ikari
Dec. 4, 2001	Birth of Asuka Soryu Langley
2002	Gendo and Fuyutsuki head to Antarctica for an official investigation into the Second Impact
	Fuyutsuki learns of Misato, who is suffering from aphasia, in the No. 2 isolation unit of the Antarctica Research Vessel
2003	Strategic Self-Defense Forces (SSDF) established as a result of a clash between China and Vietnam on the Spratly islands.
	Fuyutsuki pushes Gendo Ikari, head of the Artificial Evolution Research Institute to release the truth about the Second Impact. Gendo invites Fuyutsuki to join the team at GEHIRN

2004	Yui Ikari disappears during an experiment at the No. 2 underground research facility at Hakone
	Gendo Ikari also disappears temporarily. Upon his return he proposes the Adam Plan, a Human Completion Program. Shinji moves out and starts to live apart from Gendo.
2005	Creation of New Tokyo-3 approved by parliament and construction begun in Fuji-Hakone
	Misato Katsuragi meets Ritsuko Akagi and Ryoji Kaji at the No. 2 Tokyo University
	Asuka Soryu Langley selected as the Second Children. Kyoko Soryu Zeppelin commits suicide the very same day.
2008	Dr Naoko Akagi completes the MAGI basic theory
	Ritsuko Akagi joins GEHIRN; works on E-project
2009	Misato Katsuragi joins No. 3 German sub-branch of GEHIRN.
2010	Naoko tells Ritsuko of the MAGI, which incorporates parts of her character into the computers
	MAGI system completed
	Rei Ayanami (first generation) joins GEHIRN. Meets Ritsuko and Naoko for first time
	Dr Akagi commits suicide
	GEHIRN disbanded; NERV formed
2014	Completion of entry plug that Shinji and his friends occupy while piloting Evas
2015	Activation experiments on Eva-00 carried out at No. 2 Lab at NERV HQ. Experiments fail. Rei Ayanami suffers serious injury and Eva-00 is temporarily sealed.
	The Angels attack New Tokyo-3 for the first time in 15 years.
	Shinji is called to New Tokyo-3 by Gendo.
	The third Angel - Sachiel - destroyed by Eva-01, which has careened out of control.
	Shinji begins living with Misato.
	Attack of the fourth Angel Shamshiel.

Shinji enters the fray with Kensuke and Toji on board.

Apart from its core, an Angel is acquired in almost pristine condition.

Activation experiments recommenced on Eva-00. Experiments succeed.

Attack of the fifth Angel Ramiel.

Attack of the sixth Angel Gagiel.

Adam brought to NERV HQ by Ryoji Kaji.

Mysterious object submerged in waters off the Kii Peninsula verified as the seventh Angel Israfel.

Eighth Angel Sandalphon discovered in the crater of the Mount Asama volcano according to reports from the Asama Seismological Institute.

Misato issues special order A-17 allowing NERV to seize Sandalphon alive.

Emergence of Eva-02 equipped with a "heat-resistant, pressure-resistant, and nuclear-resistant suit along with D-type apparatus for brush-fire wars."

Experiments conducted aimed at extending the operation time for Evas, which end in failure.

Electrical power to the NERV HQ is almost totally cut off, leaving only 1.2% of capacity in operation.

Ninth Angel, Martiel, which had been thought likely to come ashore near Atami, is found.

Gendo and Fuyutsuki recover the Spear of Longinus from Antarctica.

10th Angel, Sahaquiel, emerges in an orbit above the Indian Ocean.

Misato issues special order D-17, by which all citizens are directed to evacuate the city.

Harmonics test conducted directly on the skin minus the plug suits.

87th protein wall corrodes and releases heat. 11th Angel, Ireul, found to have penetrated NERV.

Angels hack into MAGI through security computer-bank.

	Eva-00 uses Spear of Longinus for an undisclosed task.
	12th Angel, Leliel, appears in sky above New Tokyo-3.
	Decision made to drop 992 N2 mines.
	US-based NERV No. 2 sub-branch disappears during loading tests of S2 organ onto Eva-04.
	Toji Suzuhara officially informed that he is Fourth Children.
	Angel awakes in a specially constructed temporary holding pen below the Matsushiro No.2 research facility. At just that moment there is a huge explosion.
	Eva-03 officially destroyed, after being discovered to be the 13th Angel, Bardiel.
	Shinji decides to quit as Eva pilot.
	14th Angel, Zeruel, appears above the Komagatake defense line.
	Eva-01 used as bait for the Angels, gaining the S2 organ in the process.
	Beginning of salvage operations.
	Ryoji Kaji shot to death in SEELE rebellion.
	New Tokyo-3 destroyed as Eva-00 self-destructs.
	15th Angel, Ariel, attacks from satellite orbit.
	16th Angel, Armisael, attacks.
	Death of Rei Ayanami.
	Shinji meets Kaoru.
	Kaoru Nagisa destroyed after being discovered to be the 17th Angel, Tabris.
	SEELE issues orders to put Human Completion Plan into action. Japan left devastated following Third Impact.
2016	Human Completion Plan Commenced.

Neon Genesis Evangelion
The Surface

Story

It is the year 2015, and mankind uses the android Evas to fight against the mysterious Angels that threaten Earth. Shinji Ikari, Rei Ayanami and Asuka Soryu Langley, a 14-year-old girl who has lost her mother, pilot the Evas.

A special organization named NERV has been given enormous powers even while being shunned by the government. NERV, and the secret organization behind it, SEELE, set out to develop the Human Completion Plan, which will lead humanity to a new evolutionary level once the Angels have been destroyed.

However, there is a conflict of opinion over how the plan should be realized, and a full-scale military clash seems inevitable once the final Angel is defeated.

Everything depends on Shinji Ikari, a necessary component of the Human Completion Plan. After much anguish, he decides against any form of "completion."

The final Angel is destroyed in Episode 24 of the TV series, setting the stage for the movie *The End of Evangelion.*

Just what is it that powers the Evangelions? 01

It goes without saying that the Evangelions, referred to as Evas for short, are the major mechanical feature of the series. Eva is the ultimate universal fighting weapon that human beings are capable of producing. While said to be androids, the model for Eva is the Giant of Light - believed to be the first Angel Adam - which appears at the time of the Second Impact in the Antarctic in the year 2000. Beginning with Eva-00, Eva-01 and Eva-02, in total 13 Evas are planned.

The Evas are equipped with something resembling a soul, known as a "core," that is the source of their power. They are operated by signals relayed from the pilot's nervous system to the core, allowing the pilot's thoughts to be translated directly into actions.*

However, as it is impossible for the pilot to reproduce mental pictures of movements or motions that he has no experience of, a manual is included for certain operations.**

In many cases the pilot and the Evas do

See Glossary
Evangelion
Giant of Light
Angel
Second Impact
Core
Pilot

not work in perfect synch, and the system is referred to as "O9," because the failure rate is extremely high, as illustrated by a successful activation ratio of 0.000000001 percent.

The chemistry between man and machine is influenced by the compatibility between the pilot and the Eva's core. This means that if Shinji, pilot of Eva-01, attempts to pilot Eva-00, it will be impossible for him to attain an equivalent level of skill. Each Eva requires its individual, dedicated pilot.

Armaments

The Evas appear to have no fixed weaponry. They are armed with a Progressive Knife stored near the shoulder, but for the most part they are pre-mounted with arms before entering battle, depending on who or what their opponent is.

*The pilot is not required to move his legs to make the Eva walk.

** Shinji has no experience of using firearms.

See Glossary
Shinji Ikari
O9 System
Progressive Knife

What kind of substance is LCL? 02

LCL is the name of the yellow liquid that fills the Evangelion entry plug. When the pilot mounts the entry plug, his or her body becomes coated both inside and out with LCL. This is to counter the affects of acceleration, and is cited as effective in protecting the respiratory organs. As well as containing an oxygen solution that allows the pilot to breath, LCL also works as a neural-circuit, serving to communicate the thoughts of the pilot to the Eva.

There are clues to the properties of LCL. In Episode 5, a mass of bubbles forms in the entry plug of Eva-01 after it takes a direct hit from the fifth Angel's beam. This suggests that the oxygen solution has vaporized, meaning it has a relatively low boiling point. Also, in one scene, Gendo's glasses change shape after coming into contact with LCL that has leaked from the entry plug of Eva-00, suggesting that it has the quality to melt objects.

It is, however, difficult to rid ourselves of

See Glossary
LCL
Evangelion
Entry Plug
Pilot
Angel
Gendo Ikari

the feeling that the author is looking to maintain a veil of secrecy over what LCL actually is. For example, there are instances where the theories do not appear to hold true, such as when Rei takes what is left of the glasses into the entry plug of Eva-00.

There are also many cases when material entities, which are initially placed in a scientific context, are attributed with more abstract qualities.

LCL is a case in point. Later in the story it is described as the basis of all life forms. When the Third Impact takes place as a result of the Human Completion Plan, mankind reverts to LCL after the AC Field is broken. (The AC Field in itself is an extremely abstract idea; first described as a barrier, it later appears as a material border between human beings and other races.)

As with LCL, the story of Evangelion is endowed with both scientific and abstract concepts, all of which work to make it remarkably perplexing.

See Glossary
Rei Ayanami
Third Impact
Human Completion Plan
AT Field

How long can an Evangelion operate for? 03

When an Evangelion is in storage, it is fitted with an umbilical cable that supplies it with electricity, the source of its power. As long as the cable is connected an Eva can operate for any length of time. Evas also come with an internally stored battery and will operate until the power is exhausted. A battery's life depends on the kind of activities involved, but is anywhere between one and five minutes. Remaining Eva power is indicated on a flickering digital display at NERV. This shows that it is difficult to accurately display remaining power on a minute-by-minute basis as the flow of the energy fluctuates.

In Episode 19, Eva-00 acquires perpetual energy after it eats the S2 - super solenoid - organ of the 14th Angel Zeruel. It now no longer needs a wired power source, and can operate freely. However, it isn't until the second half of the story that Eva-00 can operate without time limitations.

See Glossary
Evangelion
Umbilical Cable
NERV
Angel
S2 organ
Zeruel

EVA Profile 001

Name **Shinji Ikari**

Pilot of Eva-01, and Third Children. Son of Gendo Ikari, Supreme Commander of NERV
Age: 14
NERV ID: 0001-137-22
Date of Birth: June 6, 2001
Blood type: A
Talents/skills/interests: Cello, housework, listening to classical music

Since losing his mother, Yui, while still young, Shinji has lived apart from his father Gendo, being raised by someone known simply as "sensei" - the master. He returns to New Tokyo-3 upon being unexpectedly summoned by Gendo, only to be thrown into the fight against the third Angel, Sachiel, without training or preparation. It's a close call, but he emerges victorious from the fight.

Originally a withdrawn, introverted kid who avoided contact with others whenever possible, Shinji wakes to the joys of being with other people and blossoms into a positive individual after he moves in with Misato and Asuka, and attends school with Toji and Kensuke. Shinji has a strong father-complex, believing himself to be unloved and unwanted, and it is praise from Gendo that persuades him to pilot the Eva. While desperate to be understood by his father, he also tries to understand Gendo. However, he is overtaken by doubt when the same man who has praised him, saying, "Well done Shinji," then turns round and attempts to kill his close friend. Gendo ends up an object of Shinji's hatred.

碇
シンジ

What are the events surrounding Yui's death? 04

Yui is the mother of the main character, Shinji. As a young woman, she is a remarkably bright biology student, able even to impress Professor Fuyutsuki, the authority on metaphysical biology, with the quality of her work.

As a result she takes part in the Adam Regeneration Project conducted by NERV in 2004. However, she is killed in an accident that occurs during the Evangelion activation tests. Remarkably, Yui's soul is somehow transplanted into Eva-01.

Gendo, Shinji's father, goes missing for a while following the accident. On his return, he shifts the entire orientation of NERV activities to a Human Completion Plan. Gendo's motivation for this is superficially explained as a selfish plan to use the Human Completion Plan to bring him closer to the soul of Yui. (There are major differences between the NERV Human Completion Plan and the SEELE plan, which is explained later.)

See Glossary
Yui Ikari
Shinji Ikari
Kozo Fuyutsuki
NERV
Adam Regeneration Plan
Evangelion
Activation
Gendo Ikari
Human Completion Plan
SEELE

At the same time, theories also exist suggesting Yui may have become one with the core of Eva-01 of her own volition. Indeed, in a later flashback scene she says, "People can only live on this planet. But Eva can live forever with the heart of a human being inside the core of the machine... Even though five billion years may pass, and the earth, the moon and the sun may disappear, I will survive. I will be lonely, but if it gives me the chance to live on..."

If we return for a moment to her academic years, it's also possible to surmise that the Human Completion Plan touted by Gendo was in fact originally the work of Yui.

The Eva-01, coupled with the soul of Yui, is the only machine capable of protecting the pilot - in this case Shinji - even if he is not at the controls, and it is treated with particular care by Gendo and his accomplices. Although Yui appears in few scenes, she occupies an important place in the development of the Evangelion story.

See Glossary
Core
Pilot

Why is Shinji chosen to pilot the Eva? 05

The first point to be made about Evangelion is that all pilots are 14-year-olds born in the year of the Second Impact. The second is the level of synchronization with the machine required of an Eva pilot. As it is the soul of Yui that is in the core of Eva-01, we can surmise that Shinji is chosen as pilot based on the belief that he will be able to achieve a high level of synchronicity with the soul of his mother.

Indeed this is the case, as even those at NERV are astounded by the rapport between pilot and Eva. It is a similar case with Eva-02, in which the soul of Kyoko, the mother of Asuka, occupies the core. Asuka is able to achieve a high level of affinity as a result.

However, this wasn't the case for the First Children, Rei Ayanami, for whom it took seven months of training to achieve synchronization with Eva-00. (We should also remember that Rei is a parentless a clone.)

When Asuka is appointed Second

See Glossary
Evangelion
Pilot
Second Impact
Shinji Ikari
Synchro-Ratio
Yui Ikari
Core
NERV
Kyoko Langley Soryu
Asuka Langley Soryu
Rei Ayanami
Children

Children, her mother Kyoko is still alive, meaning she has yet to become part of the Eva core.

This suggests that the mother-child relationship is not the absolute condition governing pilot-core affinity. In Episode 1 Shinji is called to NERV as a pilot candidate. If the mother-child relationship were such a decisive factor, there would be no reason for the Muldock Organization, more of which will be discussed later.

The fact that the pilots were born in the year of the Second Impact appears to be of much more importance. There is a theory that all the students in Shinji's year at junior high school are candidates to become Second Children.

However, if we ask why Shinji is immediately able to pilot the Eva-01, the most convincing argument is that it is because his mother Yui resides in the core.

See Glossary
Muldock Organization

See questions
1
4
8
9
14
15
41
42

What actually are the Angels? 06

The Angels are an unidentified enemy of mankind. They are self-restoring, self-evolving stand-alone weapons with learning capabilities. Their bodies have the qualities of both particles and waves, and as such are composed of quantum materials, making them effectively impossible to analyze.

The wave pattern unique to the Angels is a 99.89 percent match of human DNA. This means that the Angels hold almost all information in common with human beings. The first Angel is Adam, who, as the prototype for all human beings, illustrates how extremely close Angels are to us.

The names of the Angels are all taken from the Old Testament.

The First Angel

Unspecified

It is never spelled out in the story itself, but the most likely theory is that the gigantic flash of light that appeared at the time of the Second Impact in

See Glossary
Angel
Adam
Second Impact

Antarctica was Adam. He is therefore given the name Giant of Light. The story of Evangelion is based on Adam.

The Second Angel
Unspecified

Also never clearly spelled out in so many words in the story itself. One theory is that this is also Adam - later found to be called Lilith - who is crucified below the GeoFront - a perfectly spherical cyst-like cavern discovered in the earth below Japan. Some researchers hold to a slightly more far-fetched theory that has Ayanami as the second Angel.

The Third Angel
Sachiel: Angel of Water, Controller of Storms

As the name implies, this Angel is able to operate on either land or sea. Sachiel's external appearance is similar to humans, with something approximating a face in the upper torso.

Thanks to the AT Field, an absolute defense wall common to all Angels, Sachiel is protected from almost all existing weapons. As well as the ability to repair damage and increase performance, Sachiel has a learning function. In hand-to-hand fighting, it can seize its enemy with its long arms. The spear-like weapon stored in the forearm is used in a piston-like manner to stab opponents.

At the outset, it overpowers Eva-01 but is eventually beaten into a pulp. The machine careens out of

See Glossary
Antarctica
Giant of Light
Evangelion
Lilith
GeoFront
Rei Ayanami
Sachiel
AT Field
Out of Control

control and finally self-destructs.

The Fourth Angel

Shamshel: Chief Protector of the Garden of Eden, Angel of Day

Shamshel's exterior resembles an insect. It comprises two parts, with a disc for a head and a long abdominal section extending to the rear. It has a pair of arms, eight legs, and its core - which is the only vulnerable part of an Angel - is situated in the joint between the head and the abdomen.

Shamshel attacks with constantly moving whip-like motions. Using this, it is also able to tear apart palette rifles and armored buildings, as well as pierce the body of Eva-01. Shamshel is also seen seizing the legs of Eva-01 and throwing it. However, given that with Toji and Kensuke in the entry plug Eva-01 beats Shamshel, it is evident that it is not very powerful.

The Fifth Angel

Ramiel: Controller of Thunder and the Angel of Mercy

An octagon, its eight surfaces are smooth with high reflectivity. Ramiel has no animal-like features and is closer to an inorganic substance than an organism.

However, it is endowed with precision and instantaneous movement, whether on the offensive or counter-offensive. The accelerated particles shot from a powerful laser weapon whenever an enemy encroaches within a specific area of it can also be

See Glossary
Shamshel
Core
Palette Rifle
Toji Suzuhara
Kensuke Aida
Entry Plug
Ramiel

used against more distant targets. They have enough destructive power to pierce an armored building or melt the triple-armored chest of Eva-01. Ramiel can also produce a huge shield. With this it drills into the GeoFront barriers. Exposing few weaknesses either when attacking or defending, it is a formidable flying fortress. However, it is eventually destroyed in a joint-operation between Eva-00 and Eva-01.

The Sixth Angel
Gaghiel: Controller of Fish

An Angel specifically designed for underwater. It has a streamlined body and is capable of moving freely through water with snaking movements.

While possessing no specific assault methods, it is capable of sinking the warships of the United Nations fleet one after another by ramming them at great speed. Against opponents at close quarters, it opens wide its huge jaws and tears them apart with its sharp fangs. The core of Gaghiel is also in its mouth, but is seldom exposed.

Gaghiel is also the first Angel to appear outside New Tokyo-3. Its target is believed to be the contents of Ryoji Kaji's trunk - the Adam embryo. It is also worth noting that the fight with Gaghiel sees Eva-02 appear for the first time.

See Glossary
Gaghiel
New Tokyo-3
Ryoji Kaji
Israfel

The Seventh Angel

Israfel: Angel of the Last Judgment, Angel of the Resurrection, Patron Saint of Music

Israfel is endowed with the ability to divide and fuse. When it meets Eva-02 in battle in the ocean off the Kii Peninsula, it is split into two by the Eva's Sonic Grave spear. However, it immediately forms two separate entities that are capable of continuing the fight.

The fighting capabilities of Israfel remain high even after it divides, and it shakes off Eva-02 with relative ease. Its weaponry includes claws that are sharp enough to tear through armor plating and visible light rays for use in long-range assaults. Even if one half of the divided entity is defeated, it is capable of regeneration by fusing with the remaining half. It is believed that the only way to effectively tackle Israfel is to engage in a simultaneous attack on both cores. It is eventually destroyed not by a weapon, but with a kick.

The Eighth Angel

Sandalphon: Angel of Glory, Angel of Prayer, Angel of Embryos

Sandalphon is first discovered as a chrysalis that closely resembles a human embryo in the volcanic crater of Mount Asama. Eva-02 is sent on the first attempt to capture an Angel, but Sandalphon suddenly awakens.

See Glossary
Sandalphon
Mount Asama

Sandalphon develops at an alarming speed once hatched. It resembles an early carnivorous life-form, the primitive fish, *Anomalocaris*. In this form it swims freely through the lava, effectively playing with Eva-02. Sandalphon attacks Eva-02 with its pair of arms and a set of jaws that can open even in the heat of the lava.

Despite the fact that it is unaffected by the lava, moving with agility through the heat, once it is destroyed nothing remains. From this we can surmise that its AT Field helped it withstand the heat and pressure.

The Ninth Angel

Matriel: Angel of Rain.

The long thin legs that extend from Matriel's body closely resemble those of a spider, although there are only four of them. While there are many eye-like apertures in Matriel's oval body, it appears that they are used to create a chameleon-like camouflage. The largest of these apertures oozes a powerful solution that Matriel probably uses to infiltrate the barriers of GeoFront, and with which it manages to stall Eva-03.

In the end, Matriel is defeated with relative ease by a coordinated attack of three Evas.

The 10th Angel

Sahaquiel: One of the seven great Archangels listed in the Third Book of Enoch, Guardian of the Fourth Heaven and Lord of the Sky

Sahaquiel is the angel that first appears in an orbit over the earth. Many times bigger than the Evas,

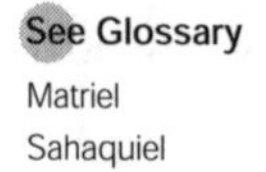

Sahaquiel is huge even when compared to other Angels. It has a symmetrical form similar to amoeba. It pounds the earth with chunks from its own body, dropping them to Earth where they detonate on impact. After breaking off from the main body, each object becomes a separate and unique organism. As they drop, these "bombs" increase in destructivity by developing AT Fields.

Sahaquiel finally drops in an attempt to destroy New Tokyo-3. The main part of the Angel also manages to expand its AT Field in space destroying a search satellite.

The 11th Angel

Ireul: Angel of Fear

Ireul operates as a colony of bacteria-size organisms. It evolves at explosive speeds, and is incredibly difficult to fight off as it thrives on the weaknesses of its opponents.

With each separate microscopic unit able to develop its own AT Field, Ireul's ultimate aim is to hack into the super-computer MAGI, the very brain of NERV. It achieves this by transforming itself into something close to an electrical circuit, becoming a being with both organic and program-based characteristics.

Ireul succeeds in hacking into the Melchior and Balthasar areas of the MAGI system, but fails in its aim of defeating NERV by inducing the system to self-destruct. It cannot fully contaminate the final level,

See Glossary
Ireul
Colonies
MAGI System
NERV

Casper, and thus gain total coordination between all three areas, the perquisite for MAGI's self-destruction.

The 12th Angel

Leliel: Angel of the Night, Prince of Conception

Leliel apparently comprises the orb that appears in the sky over New Tokyo-3 and the shadow it casts on the ground. The orb is in fact a shadow and the main body of the angel.

It has a diameter of 680 meters and a thickness of approximately 3 nanometers. This ultra thin mass is externally supported by an AT Field, with the interior linked to a theoretical space known as the Dirac Sea.

Leliel approaches in silence, sucking its opponents into the darkness of anti-matter from which they cannot escape.

Eva-01 is one such victim. Shinji switches to life-support mode and awaits help. But as the power in the plug suit fades, Shinji prepares to accept his fate. Suddenly, a woman's voice calls out to him from the depths of maternal love. It is his mother Yui Ikari. This event effectively establishes the relationship between Yui and Eva-01.

The 13th Angel

Bardiel: The Angel of Hail and Lightning.

Concealing itself in thunderclouds, Bardiel manages to infect Eva-03 as a parasitical presence while it is being shipped from the US. Awakening upon activa-

See Glossary
Leliel
Plug Suit
Bardiel
Matsushiro
Activation

tion of its host during experiments at Matsushiro, Bardiel destroys the lab.

Its foremost feature is the living tissue formed of bacterial filaments that allows it to organically alter the special armor of the Eva and perform extraordinary extensions to the chest area.

It is able to draw out the capabilities of the Eva to their absolute limit, allowing it to attack at will. Its source of power is regeneration, unique to the Angels.

The other pilots are unwilling to launch an attack on Eva-03 as Toji is in the entry plug. Nor can Shinji do a thing to help and the pilots are forced on the defensive. While being strangled by the stretched and contorted limbs of Bardiel, Shinji says, "I'd sooner die than have to kill someone." And it is this lack of will to attack that causes the operating circuits of Eva-01 to switch to a dummy plug.

A scene evolves where the dummy plug becomes overwhelmingly powerful, the NERV operators are quaking with fear, and Shinji is attempting to stop the dummy plug. But his father Gendo ignores his son's requests after Shinji refuses to retaliate against Bardiel/Eva-03. The dummy plug attacks, destroying the Angel and injuring Toji when it crushes the entry plug.

The 14th Angel

Zeruel: The Angel of Might.

As its name suggests, Zeruel is the strongest Angel to

See Glossary
Toji Suzuhara
Zeruel

emerge so far. Zeruel cannot be detected on radar, and manages to infiltrate GeoFront. It easily shakes off attacks by Eva-00 and Eva-02 and achieves the first physical infiltration of Central Dogma.

Zeruel releases light rays from its skull-like head, reducing the special armored protective wall of GeoFront to dust in an instant. It throws out its tentacled arms, which it can extend and shorten at will, and slices off the arms and head of Eva-02.

Zeruel is also capable of covering its normally exposed core with a protective shell or crust at the first sign of attack. Zeruel is unscathed by Rei's and Asuka's attacks, and moves purposefully toward Central Dogma.

In the ensuing chaos, Shinji is no longer piloting the Eva, Rei almost dies in an ultimately unsuccessful attack on the Angel, and people are running for their lives. Kaji successfully persuades Shinji to again take the controls of the Eva.

Shinji attacks, but fails to notice his waning power. However, the core of Eva-01 miraculously accedes to Shinji's wishes and reactivates itself. Shinji's synchronization level with the machine reaches an incredible 400%, leading the Eva to develop new powers with which it finally destroys the Angel.

The 15th Angel

Ariel: The Angel of Birds.

Ariel at first appears in orbit over the earth in the form of a bright, shining bird-like creature. It bom-

See Glossary
Central Dogma
Ariel

bards Eva-02 with a visible wavelength energy beam that closely resembles an AT Field.

The energy beam invades the pilot's mind and burrows deep into the subconscious, causing the pilot to recall traumatic incidents from her childhood. This pushes the pilot's life-support circuits to within an inch of overload.

We can surmise that apart from nullifying the fighting capabilities of its opponent, this offensive style is a form of hacking designed to learn about the mental structure of human beings.

When Asuka's situation looks dire, Gendo orders Rei to use the Spear of Longinus. Misato protests that doing so may set off the Third Impact, but the order cannot be overruled and Misato is left feeling that everything she has learned is lies.

She takes the spear from Central Dogma, where it is thrust into Adam, and with it Eva-00 destroys the Angel, leaving Asuka's pride in tatters.

The 16th Angel

Armisael: The Angel of the Womb.

Armisael has no permanent structure. A disc when it first appears, it changes into a cord-like being when Eva-00 seeks to intercept it. It attacks Eva-00 with the tip of the cord, while setting of a process of physical fusion with the connecting portion of the cord.

Armisael hacks into the psyche of the pilot, attempting a communications-based attack. While launching an attack on Eva-01, Armisael transforms itself

See Glossary
Spear of Longinus
Third Impact
Armisael

into the external appearance of the pilot of Eva-00, setting off a similar fusion.

Armisael communicates with Rei, tapping into her loneliness and her desire to be with Shinji and making her believe it can make all this happen. However, Rei realizes this ruse, and in a last-ditch attempt to save Shinji holds down Armisael, self-destructing along with New Tokyo-3.

The 17th Angel

Kaoru Nagisa/Tabris

Kaoru is the Angel that immediately brings Shinji under his power. Why is Kaoru the only Angel with a human form and heart? Why is it that the MAGI cannot identify it? There are too many unknowns and too many mysteries surrounding Kaoru.

See Glossary
Tabris
Kaoru Nagisa
Lilim

See questions
1 2 7 8
9 10 12 16
21 28 37 41
42

The 18th Angel

Human beings/Lilims

EVA Profile 002

Name **Rei Ayanami**

Pilot of the prototype Eva-00,
and First Children. The first person to be
selected by the Nulodck Organization.
Age: 14
NERV ID: 0001-225-09
Date of Birth: Unknown
Blood type: Unknown
Interests: Reading

Rei is a cloned human being. Her cell donor is believed to be Yui - mother of Shinji. Still, when we consider that Rei has no reproductive capabilities and that in Episode 24 she generates an AT Field herself, we can see that she is no ordinary clone, but has a very mysterious presence. A girl of few words, who is unable to express her emotions, Rei underestimates her value to the world, and is unable to drum up anger even if openly insulted or abused. But this is the same girl who slaps Shinji across the face just for saying that he does not believe in his father - Gendo. She also flashes her anger at Asuka for criticizing Shinji. At the start of the story, Rei is unable to open her heart to anyone except Gendo Ikari, but begins to blossom as a human being from her relationship with Shinji. It must be remembered that this is the third incarnation of Rei; the first having being killed by Naoko Akagi, the second self-destructs as she attempts to save Shinji in Episode 23.

Rei's popularity soared in Japan, with books featuring her image on the cover selling like hot cakes. She was christened by the media, "The girl who manipulates magazine sales at will," "The fastest route to the sold-out sign!" And even, "The Premium Girl."

綾波レイ

EVA Profile 003

Name **Asuka Langley Soryu**

Pilot of Eva-02, and Second Children.
Of US nationality, but with some German and Japanese blood. Appears from Episode 8.
Age: 14
NERV ID: 0001-225-09
Date of Birth: December 4, 2001
Blood type: O
Talents/skills/interests: Swearing at people, piloting Eva and video games.

Asuka arrives in Japan from Germany along with Eva-02 and Ryoji Kaji. En route, they are attacked by the sixth Angel, Gagiel. She manages to fight off Gagiel and win her first battle against the Angels thanks to Shinji, who is in the entry plug of Eva-02. Asuka is independent and outward going; she is proud and always wants to be the center of attention. She mercilessly wipes out all who stand in her way, and is forever looking down on those around her. She is a prodigy, having graduated from a German university, but remains very much a child.

The truth may well be that having depicted Rei as too much of an introvert, the creators went the other way with Asuka and made her overly gregarious.

Asuka's mother commits suicide after being contaminated by the spirit of the Eva, the cause of much trauma for Asuka. Being an Eva pilot is the source of great pride to Asuka, but her trauma is sparked by her feelings of defeat toward Shinji and the psychological attack from the 15th Angel, Ariel. This leads to a nervous breakdown that leaves her incapable of even starting up her Eva. She may be the most tragic of the characters in Evangelion.

惣流

アスカ・ラングレー

What is the AT Field? 07

The Absolute Terror Field appears to be an area enclosed by a phase-transition space. The field can decide whether heat, magnetic waves and dynamic energy pass through or are screened. The field cannot be destroyed either with conventional weaponry or nuclear arms.

In the first half of the Evangelion story, the AT Field is described as a barrier unique to the Angels. As all the Angels use the field as basic protection, it is impossible to attack them from a distance using lasers. This requires their attackers to engage in close-quarter combat, the reason why the Evas use such weapons as knives when attacking the Angels.

The eighth Angel - Sandalphon - is able to withstand extremely high temperatures and pressure of lava. However, it disappears without a trace immediately its AT Field is removed. This suggests that the AT Field is also effective against high temperatures.

There are instances of AT Fields interfer-

See Glossary
Evangelion
AT Field
Angel
Sandalphon

ing with each other, or of them transforming or disappearing all together. In Episode 6 it is proved that the field can be penetrated, after 180 million kilowatts of power are focused at a single point above it.

In the latter half of the story, we learn that the AT Field is not unique to the Angels, but is closer to being the power generated by the soul. This means that all of us are capable of producing the field. In Kaoru's words, taken from Episode 24, "It is a sacred zone that must not be sullied by anybody...The light of the heart...The walls of the heart that we all possess."

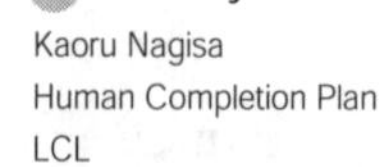

Kaoru Nagisa
Human Completion Plan
LCL

It becomes apparent later that the purpose of the Human Completion Plan is to remove the AT Field from all human beings and turn them into LCL - in other words, liquid.

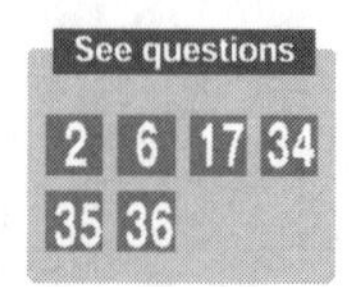

What kind of organization is NERV? 08

NERV could be described as the allied military organization. Its full title is Special Organ NERV, and it is under the direct control of the United Nations. "NERV" itself appears to come from the German word for "nerve" or "vein." The supreme commander of NERV is Gendo Ikari and vice commander is Kozo Fuyutsuki.

NERV HQ is in New Tokyo-3, with Sub-sections 1 and 2 in the US and a third sub-section in Germany. Other branches are dotted around the world. The main mission of NERV is to maintain and operate the Evangelions while researching and destroying the Angels.

NERV HQ is a pyramid-like building in the center of GeoFront, which is situated below New Tokyo-3. In Central Dogma, located deep within GeoFront, is a living creature that has been crucified. This is Adam, or at least it is believed to be the Adam that has grown from the embryo that appears in Episode 8. However, it is later discovered to be Lilith.

See Glossary
NERV
Gendo Ikari
Kozo Fuyutsuki
New Tokyo-3
Evangelion
Angel
GeoFront
Central Dogma
Adam
Lilith

The armored buildings of New Tokyo-3, at a higher level than GeoFront, are laid out in the form of a crucifix.

Misato Katsuragi belongs to the No. 1 Section of the Tactical Bureau, and has overall authority for leading the fight against the Angels.

In Episode 6 we learn that her authority is almost without limits. In order to defeat the fifth Angel, she commandeers weaponry from the Self-Defense Forces and uses the nation's entire electricity supply.

The ultimate aim of NERV is to defeat all the Angels and prevent the occurrence of the Third Impact, which was prophesized in the Dead Sea Scrolls. However, this is only its official purpose. The real aim of NERV and the mysterious organization that supports it - SEELE, controlled by Keel Lorentz - is the implementation of the Adam Regeneration Plan and the Human Completion Plan.

It is later revealed that the Evangelions were produced based on the Adam Regeneration Plan. We also discover that in order to put the Human Completion Plan into operation, it is necessary to bring about the Third Impact. In other words, the official purpose of NERV and its true purpose are diametrically opposed.

See Glossary
Misato Katsuragi
Third Impact
Secret Dead Sea Scrolls
SEELE
Keel Lorentz
Adam Regeneration Plan
Human Completion Plan

See questions
6 11 12 17
18 19 34 35
36 38 42

What is the Second Impact that occurs in 2000 AD? 09

Second Impact generally refers to the massive meteorite that fell on Antarctica in the year 2000 and the huge explosion that followed in its wake. The ice of Antarctica melted as a result of the explosion and many of the world's cities were lost under the rising sea levels. The explosion was of such force that it appears to have twisted the earth off its axis.

According to *Second Impact*, the movie within the anime, the meteor was tens of millimeters in diameter and is described as travelling close to the speed of light when it smashed into Antarctica. As a result, half of humanity was destroyed, the eco-system was knocked out of kilter, the four seasons disappeared leaving the heat of summer to be experienced all year round. In the scenes where the Evas appear, the sound of cicadas can usually be heard in the background.

However, this story of a meteorite hitting the Antarctic is a unified attempt at information manipulation by the governments of the

See Glossary
Second Impact
Antarctica

world. It is revealed that the explosion was in fact due to the collision with Antarctica of the giant - the first Angel - that is discovered there.

It appears that any contact between the Angel Adam and all following Angels sets off powerful explosions. This may also be manipulation of information by NERV, as the truth is never revealed. The basis of the story is that the Evangelions are fighting to prevent the Third Impact (an explosion with enough power to wipe out Antarctica all over again) and the Angels are attacking New Tokyo-3 with the aim of multiplying.

However, in the latter part of the story, we discover that there is a strong possibility that the Second Impact was caused by humans and that the First Impact is the Giant Impact, thought to be the meteorite that destroyed the dinosaurs.

See Glossary
Angel
Adam
NERV
Evangelion
Third Impact
New Tokyo-3
First Impact

Who or what is the first Angel Adam? 16

Adam is the gigantic flash of light that appears at the time of the Second Impact in Antarctica. His silhouette perfectly mirrors that of the Evangelions and he has a round core in the middle of his chest.

Adam first appears in Episode 8 - *Asuka Strikes!* - when the Adam that Ryoji Kaji has brought back from Germany is reduced to an embryo so small it can fit into a brief case and be carried around. Although it doesn't move, the embryo is supposedly alive.

NERV commander Gendo describes Adam as being the first human being, and it is from Episode 8 that the story of Evangelion begins to take on its famed mysteriousness.

The place where Adam develops as a pale, living organism crucified on a cross is called Central Dogma, deep within the earth below GeoFront. To quote Ritsuko from Episode 23 - *Tear/Rei III* - "In the year 2000, we paid the price for discovering God, on top of which he went and disappeared. But this

See Glossary
Adam
Second Impact
Antarctica
Evangelion
Core
Asuka Langley Soryu
Ryoji Kaji
NERV
Gendo Ikari
Central Dogma
GeoFront
Ritsuko Akagi

time we have tried to resurrect God on our own...and that is Adam."

Because we know of the Adam Regeneration Plan, we are left wondering whether the embryonic Adam raised in GeoFront might not be the same Adam of the Adam Regeneration Plan.

Elsewhere, we learn, "That which was born of Adam is the Eva," effectively proving that Adam was the model for the Evangelions.

There is also the fact that in Episode 44, much later in the series, we learn from Kaoru that the thing crucified deep in the earth below GeoFront is actually Lilith. That only serves to heighten the mystery surrounding Adam.

See Glossary
Adam Regeneration Plan
Kaoru Nagisa
Lilith

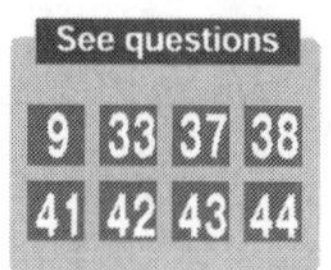

See questions
9 33 37 38
41 42 43 44

Who or what then is Lilith? 11

According to existing rabbinical texts, Lilith was the first wife of Adam. She was the incarnation of the devil, and was cast out by Adam after refusing to be an obedient wife and follower.

The role of Lilith in Evangelion is as the pale living thing, originally thought to be Adam, that is crucified deep in the earth below GeoFront. This is what we are told by the 17th Angel Kaoru. Lilith has a spear struck deep into her breast - the Spear of Longinus.

What this then signifies is that the Adam that Ryoji Kaji brought back from Germany in Episode 8 is in fact Lilith.

Kaoru refers to human beings as Lilim. Lilim is said to be the daughter of Lilith, therefore mankind was born of Lilith crucified in GeoFront. If Lilith is the incarnation of the devil, it means her offspring - mankind - are also devils.

In other words, the Adam Regeneration Plan is aimed at the eventual return to the

See Glossary
Lilith
Adam
GeoFront
Angel
Kaoru Nagisa
Spear of Longinus
Ryoji Kaji
Lilim
Adam Regeneration Plan

womb of all devils produced by Lilith. This, in essence, is the SEELE plan. Gendo's vision, however, is entirely different.

The discovery that Lilith is a separate being to Adam leads to the theory that Lilith may be the second Angel, whose presence is not explained in the Evangelion story.

See Glossary
SEELE
Gendo Ikari

See questions
6
10
17
21
33
34
35
36
38

What is New Tokyo-3? 12

New Tokyo-3 is a planned city under construction on the shores of Lake Ashi and the stage on which the Evangelion story unfolds.

The storyline has Tokyo and its environs completely wiped out by the new N2 bombs as a result of the military clash of September 20, 2000 following the Second Impact.

Also, as the Antarctic ice melted following the Second Impact, the rising sea levels left much of present day Tokyo submerged, making it impossible to reconstruct the city on its present site. It is decided at an emergency summit meeting to build a new capital in Matsumoto in Nagano Prefecture. This is New Tokyo-2.

Restoration and reconstruction work proceeds in the wake of the Second Impact, and New Tokyo-2 is serving as Japan's capital by the start of 2003. This is followed by a 2004 parliamentary decision on the Second Capital Relocation Plan, launching construction of a

See Glossary
New Tokyo-3
N2 bomb
Second Impact
Antarctica

planned city on the shores of Lake Ashi.

The condominium that Misato lives in and the junior high school Shinji attends are all in New Tokyo-3. While the city is only some two kilometers in diameter, it has a complete rail system and in the present day of 2015 has seven fully developed loop lines.

In terms of location, the city is situated in an area between present-day Hakone-Kojiri, Ohakone and Sengokubara, with Lake Ashi to the south. In the opening sequence, the sun appears to the south of New Tokyo-3, despite the fact that it is evening. This is possibly to highlight the shift in the earth's axis in the wake of the Second Impact.

New Tokyo-3 also comes with its own underground city in the form of GeoFront, the home of NERV. Here there is a pyramid, and while it remains unclear, the entire underground area appears to be the remains of a civilization left behind by an indigenous race. Of the hemispherical space, six kilometers in diameter and 0.9 kilometers in height, 89 percent is now buried.

Sunlight is channeled into the facility via optical fibers connected to a light-condensing block on the surface, making the underground area as bright as the surface.

See Glossary
Misato Katsuragi
Shinji Ikari
GeoFront
NERV
Central Dogma

See questions
8 9 10 11
37 38 41 42
44

What is the Penguin kept by Misato? 13

The Onsen Penguin kept as a pet by Misato is called PenPen. It is a new breed of penguin that lives in a freezer and likes hot springs and beer. Not only does it have claws, but it also reads the newspaper and can take its own bath!

PenPen is Misato's pet, but it is Shinji that does much of the work taking care of it. It's never really clear if Misato really likes PenPen. For its part, PenPen seems to sympathize with Shinji for being given the run-around by Misato.

We are also left wondering why a penguin, an animal that is supposed to like the cold, relishes hot baths. We can only suppose that there must be some connection between the emergence of this new breed of penguins and the Second Impact that melted the Antarctic ice.

PenPen's role is very much as a comic mascot character. However, his existence is just one more of the many elements of Evangelion that remain unexplained.

See Glossary
Misato Katsuragi
PenPen
Shinji Ikari
Second Impact
Antarctica

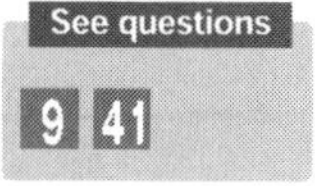

EVA Profile 004

Name **Kaoru Nagisa** **(The 17th Angel, Tabris)**

Eva-02 pilot and Fifth Children.
Sent in by the Human Completion Project Committee.
Age: 15
NERV ID: Unknown
Date of Birth: September 13, 2000
Blood type: Unknown

The last Angel (besides Lilim), Kaoru is sent to NERV by SEELE. Outwardly he is a human being, but on closer examination he possesses capabilities that far outstrip the average person. He pilots Eva-02 in place of Asuka, who has suffered a nervous breakdown, and stuns onlookers with his amazingly high synchro-ratio. He befriends Shinji, exhibiting a telepathy that has homosexual overtones. He later attempts contact with Eva-02 and Adam in Terminal Dogma after he realizes that it is Lilith and not Adam who is deep in the ground. With this, Kaoru's entire approach changes, and he chooses to die by being crushed by Eva-01 piloted by Shinji.

渚
カヲル

What is the Muldock Organization? 14

The Muldock Organization sets the standards for choosing potential Eva pilots, though for all intents and purposes it is fully under the control of, and the same entity as, NERV.

As with much of Evangelion, it is never made clear what exactly are the standards and how prospective pilots are discovered. While it may have been necessary to establish such an organization in the early stages of Eva development, as the story proceeds, the necessary conditions for, and qualities of, pilots becomes clearer, removing much of the reason for the existence of the organization.

The required qualities of a pilot are understood as the problems existing between the Eva cores and the pilots come under the spotlight. This results in the inclusion of a mother's soul in the core of the Evas to exponentially increase the synchro-ratio between pilot and machine.

See Glossary
Muldock Organization
Evangelion
Pilot
NERV
Shinji Ikari
Core
Synchro-Ratio

EVA Profile 005

Name **Toji Suzuhara**

Pilot of Eva-03, and Fourth Children.
Member of class A year 2 at the No. 1 Municipal Junior High School in New Tokyo-3, where he is a classmate and friend of Shinji.
Age: 14
NERV ID: 0254762
Date of Birth: December 26, 2001
Blood type: B
Talents: Basketball
Interests: Eating boxed lunches (bento)

鈴原トウジ

Toji's younger sister is injured as a result of the "E-incident" involving Eva-00. As a result, Toji's first reaction is to hold a grudge against Shinji and try to beat him up. However, when the fourth Angel, Shamshel, attacks he jumps into the entry plug of Eva-01, only to realize the kind of suffering that Shinji goes through each time he mounts the Eva. This leads him to befriend Shinji along with the class nerd Kensuke Aida.

In Episode 17 Toji is selected as Fourth Children and, with his younger sister in mind, agrees to become a pilot on the condition that he can transfer her to the NERV hospital. But the Eva-03 craft that he is meant to pilot is contaminated and taken over by the 13th Angel, Bardiel, while in shipment from the US. Eva-03 is knocked-out by Eva-01, which has been booted up by the dummy-system while Toji is onboard, resulting in him losing his left leg.

What do First, Second and Third Children mean? 15

In the world of the Evangelion, "Children" is a word used to denote those suitable to become pilots. They are selected from among girls and boys of 14 years of age by the previously mentioned Muldock Organization. Rei Ayanami was the first to be selected, and is therefore "First Children." It follows that Asuka Langley Soryu, the second to be selected, is "Second Children," and Shinji Ikari "Third Children."

However, these numbers do not necessarily correlate with the numbers of the Eva the characters pilot, as is shown by the fact that "Third Children" Shinji pilots the Eva-01.

One other point that rankles is that while the pilots are individuals, they are referred to not as "Child" in the singular, but "Children" in the plural. No reason is ever given for this, but among Eva followers and spoilers there is a tendency to refer to Shinji as he appears in Episode 1 as a "Reservist."

As Rei, Asuka and Shinji are all children

See Glossary
Evangelion
Children
Pilot
Muldock Organization
Rei Ayanami
Asuka Langley Soryu
Shinji Ikari

who may or may not become pilots depending on the decision of the Muldock Organization, we are led to believe that there have been other "Children" that the organization has researched but rejected as pilots.

Suppositions aside, what probably happened is that in line with the trend seen in many Japanese animated series, specific English words were picked up for their sound or tone and have little relation to their original meanings or usage.

In the latter part of the story, Toji is nominated as "Fourth Children" and Kaoru Nagisa appears as "Fifth Children," completing the five sets of children who appear in the story.

See Glossary
Toji Suzuhara
Kaoru Nagisa

Who created the super-computer - MAGI? 16

MAGI is the ultimate in NERV technology. The program was designed by Naoko Akagi, the mother of Ritsuko Akagi, and is said to contain remnants of Naoko's personality.

It is believed that the powers of the MAGI system far outstrip the capabilities of any of the Neural Network Systems - which employ learning and judgment functions based on the human nervous system - under development at present. MAGI is judged to be so advanced that its circuits and elements are aligned in much the same way as the human brain. In Episode 13, when Ritsuko examines one of MAGI's circuits, we see that its design is modeled on the human brain.

Interestingly, despite the amount of circuitry on display, it is worth noting that Ritsuko herself is in normal, everyday clothing. Any computer with that kind of processing capability could be expected to give off enormous amounts of heat, leaving us to wonder

See Glossary
MAGI
NERV
Naoko Akagi
Ritsuko Akagi

whether Ritsuko would in fact require special clothing.

When seen from the present level of advancement in computer science, we can only suppose that the quantitative and molecular devices - circuits that are configured as molecular devices themselves - use ultra high-speed technology.

MAGI is configured from three CPUs, appropriately named after the three wise men - Balthasar, Melchior and Casper.

See questions
8 30

What is the Human Completion Plan? 17

"Human Completion Plan" is one of the key terms in Evangelion, appearing again and again throughout the drama. It is somewhat odd, therefore, that it is never fully explained.

The nuanced meaning is of taking humanity, with all its shortcomings, and creating perfection from it. However, no explanation is immediately presented as to why this is necessary or why it is done. The full picture is presented later in the story, but it is a complex proposal - abstract at best - with an underpinning of religiosity.

Put in simple terms, it is accepted that God will punish selfish human beings who overstep their bounds by believing they can bring themselves closer to God by slavish devotion to science. Hence, the plan is aimed at making mankind repent for its sins and begin over again before God has the opportunity to unleash his wrath upon the earth.

To implement the plan it is necessary to

See Glossary
Human Completion Plan
Evangelion

artificially set off the Third Impact and destroy the AT Field of all mankind, and the Angel Adam/Lilith and the Evangelions based on Adam are necessary to do this.

SEELE runs NERV based on these beliefs and directs Gendo to conduct research. However, Gendo has his own Human Completion Plan in mind - which basically envisages human beings becoming Gods - and it is the gap between these two plans that forms the final focal point of the story.

The Human Completion Plan is one of many examples that show Evangelion to be not so much a Sci-Fi tale of robot derring-do, but one of unfolding religiously oriented abstract concepts. And the storyline, which appears to be difficult to follow on first viewing, may be aimed at prompting us to view the series repeatedly and dig deeper if we are to savor the mysterious fruits of Evangelion.

See Glossary
Third Impact
AT Field
Angel
Adam
Lilith
SEELE
NERV
Gendo Ikari

See questions
6 7 10 33
34 35 36 37
38 42

What is the role of the Dead Sea Scrolls in Evangelion?

SEELE is the most mysterious organization to appear in Evangelion. To uncover the mystery that veils SEELE, it is important to know something of the Dead Sea Scrolls. However, only one part of the scrolls has been made public, creating as many mysteries as the scrolls are purported to have solved.

Discovered near the Dead Sea in Israel in February 1947, the scrolls are a vast body of written work closely related to the Bible. It is said they were deposited in the caves of the barren hills surrounding the Dead Sea by the Essenes, a separatist Jewish sect of the Second Temple Period, members of which had formed an ascetic monastic community, the Qumran.

As a result of excavations and surveys, remains of the sect have also been unearthed, leading some to refer to the scrolls as the "Essene Scrolls." The commonly believed theory is that there is no direct link between the Qumran community and early Christianity.

However, some scholars highlight the sim-

See Glossary
SEELE
Secret Dead Sea Scrolls

ilarities between beliefs and practices outlined in Qumran literature and those of early Christians, including baptism, communal meals and property rights. Most interesting is the parallel organizational structures: the sectarians divided themselves into twelve tribes led by twelve chiefs, similar to the structure of the early church that had twelve apostles who, according to Jesus, would sit on twelve thrones to judge the twelve tribes of Israel.

The scrolls remain a thing of mystery. However, SEELE treats them as its personal property, as can be seen from such language as "According to the SEELE Dead Sea Scrolls, there is one more Angel to come," from Episode 23.

From this it is possible for us to postulate two theories. One, that SEELE has managed to excavate and obtain the remaining Dead Sea Scrolls, which are now in their possession. Two, that SEELE is directly descended from the Qumran community. Given that the descriptions of SEELE have strong religious undertones, the latter would appear to be the more likely of the two.

See Glossary
Angel

Either way, this would put the Dead Sea Scrolls in the hands of SEELE, allowing it to monopolize the ancient secrets. As the rightful keepers of the scrolls and deep believers in their contents, it is likely that SEELE members

attempt to realize everything written in them. According to the Evangelion storyline, the Dead Sea Scrolls prophesize that the Angels - the enemy - will appear in the year 2015, and that mankind will be annihilated in an explosion, known as the Third Impact.

This aim of SEELE, with its deeply religious connotations, is to recreate the world in line with the prophecies of the scrolls.

SEELE aims to use Lilith and the Evas to spark the Third Impact to wipe out of much of mankind and allow the evolution of a new strain of human being. This, in essence, is the Human Completion Plan.

Destroying humanity in the name of humanity may smack of religious zealotry, but it does show us that SEELE believes it has a natural right to lead and control events.

Third Impact
Lilith
Human Completion Plan

EVA Profile 006

Name **Kensuke Aida**

Member of class A year 2 at the No. 1 Municipal Junior High School in New Tokyo-3, where his classmate and friend is Shinji.
Pilot of Eva-03, and Fourth Children.
Age: 14
NERV ID: 0257031
Date of Birth: September 12, 2001
Blood type: A
Talents: 3DCAD
Interests: Military goods in any shape or form

相田
ケンスケ

One of Evangelion's Three Stooges and a sucker for anything of a military nature, Kensuke will willingly goof off from school to see any warship that comes in. He seems to have a father, who is connected with NERV, but no mother. He is an open kid with a healthy curiosity that sometimes leads him to stick his nose in where it's not wanted. His dream is to become an Eva pilot.

Name **Hikari Horaki**

Class Rep. of class A year 2.
Age: 14
Date of Birth: February 18, 2002
Blood type: AB
Talents: Cooking
Interests: Cooking

洞木
ヒカリ

Hikari is the responsible bossy type, and it is no surprise that she takes control of the class. Because of this, she often gets on her classmates nerves. She christens Shinji, Toji and Kensuke, "The Three Stooges."

What is the United Nations Force? 19

The United Nations Force referred to in Evangelion comprises tank brigades and a Pacific fleet, the sum of which makes it a vastly superior fighting force to the current UN peacekeeping forces. However, it is entirely ineffective against the Angels.

Given that the UN Force has bases in such locations as Atsugi and Iruma, just as the Japanese Self-Defense Force does today, there is a strong possibility that the UN Force may be a revamped international fighting force with the JSDF as the lead.

When we look at the story of Evangelion, the organization that most resembles the JSDF is the Japan Strategic Self-Defense Force Laboratory at Tsukuba, which is controlled by the Defense Ministry and is involved in the development of the Jet Alone Project.

See Glossary
Angel
Jet Alone

EVA Profile 007

Name **Misato Katsuragi**

Head of military operations at NERV, with the rank of major.
Age: 29
NERV ID: 02432-18
Date of Birth: December 8, 1985
Blood type: A
Talents: Chugging beers, driving
Interests: Driving

Given the task of destroying the Angels, Misato is also the direct commander of the Eva pilots. Being a woman in no way prevents her from coming up with audaciously bold strategies that play a major role in the destruction of the Angels. Misato is the life of the party, and has a lifestyle that sees her happily quaffing beer from first thing in the morning. She is also a bit of a slob.
Misato enjoys living together with Shinji and Asuka, but she is unable to understand Shinji at first, which leads to some friction. Once she gets to know him, she becomes quite protective. In the role of big sister and mother she develops high hopes for his development, and looks out for him when she can.

Misato experienced the Second Impact while on the Katsuragi Expedition to the South Pole, led by her father. She emerged as the only survivor after her father sacrifices his own life to save her. This experience becomes the source of her trauma, as she has difficulty coming to terms with her late father, who chose work over his family. This trauma manifests itself through her losing the power of speech in the immediate aftermath of the Second Impact.

Misato has been friends with Ritsuko Akagi and Ryoji Kaji since university, and takes up with Ryoji after they meet again.

葛城ミサト

What is the gigantic Jet Alone robot? 28

"Jet Alone" is the name given to the gigantic robot produced at the Japan Strategic Self-Defense Force Laboratory at Tsukuba. It is designed to fight the Angels and make up for the weaknesses of the Evas, given the fact that their pilots are 14-year-olds, problems are inherent in the synchro-ratio system.

Touted as being controlled externally and therefore being totally at the mercy of its makers, Jet Alone does in fact go berserk during experiments.

However, this proves to be the result of a plot by NERV, which is against the development of the Jet Alone Program.

If Jet Alone were put into practical use, it would diminish the importance of the Eva project and lead parliament to view NERV as redundant. If this were to happen, NERV would lose not only its budget - which dwarfs that of the state itself - but also many of its privileges, including its right to operate in total secrecy.

See Glossary

Jet Alone
Angel
Evangelion
Pilot
Synchro-Ratio
NERV

EVA Profile 008

Name **Ritsuko Akagi**

Systems administrator and head of the Technology Department at NERV.
Age: 30
NERV ID: Unknown
Date of Birth: November 21, 1984
Blood type: B
Interests: Addicted to coffee and cigarettes

Ritsuko is the daughter of Dr Naoko Akagi, the scientist who developed the MAGI system. She joined GEHIRN, the predecessor of NERV, straight out of university, taking over administration of the MAGI system and development of the Evas following her mother's death. She is an extremely logical character and seldom shows her emotions.

Ritsuko has been friends with Misato from university, and she supports her in both public and private. At the same time she is privy to classified information, and because of this she is acquainted with the darker goings-on at NERV. Ritsuko ends up destroying the stockpile of Rei Ayanami clones after losing her grip on life, the result of her affair with Gendo ending. Her mother was also Gendo's lover.

赤木リツコ

What is the Spear of Longinus? 21

Longinus was the name of the soldier who stabbed the already crucified Jesus with his spear, killing Him as a result.

The spear appears in Episode 4, when Gendo and Fuyutsuki retrieve it from the Antarctic. Eva-00, piloted by Rei Ayanami, transports the spear to Central Dogma. When it next appears it is protruding from the breast of the living entity held in the depths of GeoFront.

The Spear of Longinus, it appears, is a necessary element of the Human Completion Plan. But Gendo uses it to destroy Ariel, the 15th Angel that's hovering in orbit over Earth. As a result, the spear transcends the earth's atmosphere and goes into orbit around the moon, making it virtually impossible to recover.

This makes it increasingly difficult to implement the Human Completion Plan, which in turn is greeted with disappointment from Keel Lorentz and SEELE. However, Gendo has his own Human Completion Plan in mind,

See Glossary
Spear of Longinus
Gendo Ikari
Kozo Fuyutsuki
Antarctica
Rei Ayanami
Central Dogma
GeoFront
Human Completion Plan
Ariel
Angel
Keel Lorentz
SEELE

entirely different in nature to that of SEELE, and it is in line with this that he has deliberately placed the spear out of reach.

It is from this point in the Evangelion story that the differences in the two plans are highlighted. In the final episode, the spear turns up in the hands of Eva-01, proving perhaps the inevitability of the Third Impact as prophesized in the Dead Sea Scrolls.

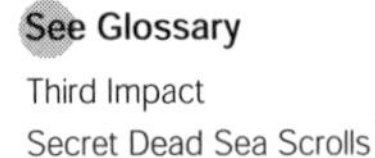

See Glossary
Third Impact
Secret Dead Sea Scrolls

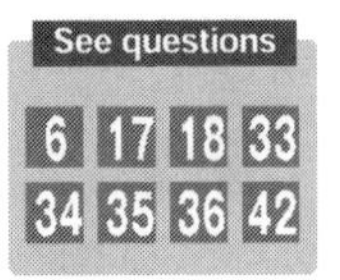

The actual Spear of Longinus can be viewed at the Cathedral of St. Augustine in Rome.

What are the unexplained images in the opening credits?

22

Most Evangelion fans that have watched the TV series from start to finish will know there are numerous unsolved mysteries in the opening credits. For example, why is it that the face of Kaoru Nagisa doesn't appear again until Episode 24?

Another such image is of what resembles a tree. This is the Inverted Tree of Life, which appears in the Kabbalah, the ancient and modern system of Jewish theosophy, mysticism and thaumaturgy, which is marked by a belief in creation through emanation and a cipher method of interpreting Scripture.

"Kabbalah" is Hebrew for "that which is received" and refers to a secret oral tradition of teaching not normally revealed to the general public.

In legend, God taught the Kabbalah to a number of angels, who, after the Fall, taught it to Adam. The Kabbalah was to help humankind to return to God. It then passed to Noah, Abraham and Moses. Eventually, the oral tradition ended

See Glossary
Kaoru Nagisa
Tree of Life
Kabbalah

and the knowledge was written down.

God is also described as "Em-Sof" ("without end"). God is unknowable beyond representation. He created the world out of himself. The chief aim of humankind is to achieve complete union with the Divine. All things are reflected in a higher world, and nothing is independent of everything else. "Thus human beings, by elevating their souls to unite with God, also elevate all other entities in the cosmos."

Throughout the opening sequences of Evangelion we are faced with numerous female nudes, and are reminded of the close relationship between sex and death.

The fact that the image of the crucifix also makes frequent appearances is meant to impress upon us the strong religious and particularly Christian-based links and allusions that appear throughout Evangelion. However, after hinting at these connections in the opening credits and early episodes, religion takes a backseat to Sci-Fi.

When Evangelion first came out, the opening was said to be unclear, or merely aimed at making a visual impact with little or no connection to the logic of the storyline. Many fans that sat through the entire series were therefore surprised to find that everything that appeared in the story had been highlighted, flagged or hinted at in the opening sequence.

See Glossary
Adam

See questions
6 33

Is it true that Evangelion is peppered with quotes from other anime? 23

Many people who have watched Evangelion with more than a passing interest have noted how the series somehow incorporates practically all the techniques used in previous anime.

Much has to do with the director Hideaki Anno. Prior to Evangelion, Anno directed such works as *Gunbuster, Aim for the Top* and *Fushigi no Umi no Nadia*. These contained rehashes of scenes from *Gettarobo* and *Space Battleship Yamato*, and caused quite a stir among die-hard anime fans.

Some suggested it was "just more mind-games from the animation crew." Others wrote it off as "Total plagiarism!"

Anno defended himself, saying, "There is no longer room for absolute originality in the field of anime, especially given that our generation was brought up on mass-produced anime. All stories and techniques inevitably bring with them a sense of deja vu. The only avenue of expression left open to us is to produce a

See Glossary
Evangelion

collage-like effect based on a sampling of existing works."

As well as acknowledging he "reworked" ideas, Anno said, "It's all down to the personality of the individual when it comes to the question of what ideas to choose, and how to use them."

The overall design of Evangelion calls to mind *Devilman* by Go Nagai. In fact, the whole concept of the Evas, which are made from Adam and harbor the souls of humans, can be considered borrowed from scenes from *Devilman*, where the soul of Akira Fudo is possessed by Amon, the Lord of War.

Moreover, the heavily religious undertones, the suggestion of conflict with an indigenous people, and the cosmic view that mankind may not be the ultimate being all owe something to *Devilman*.

On the other hand, the object in the center of the chest of the Evas closely resembles the color timer of *Ultraman*, while the restrictions placed on the operation period of the Evas is also Ultramanesque.

We can find myriad such examples if we choose to look carefully. However, the point that Anno makes is that the originality lies in the way these ideas have been reconstructed and represented in their Evangelion format.

See Glossary
Adam

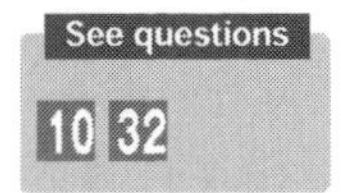

As the main character, why is Shinji so lacking in self-confidence? 24

"I mustn't run away," Shinji tells himself so many times that it's almost his trademark phrase. Although he is the main character and the pilot of an Eva, Shinji appears to have little self-confidence. This must irk a lot of Evangelion fans.

Why has the creator made this wimp of a kid the lead character?

Part of the answer may be found in the fact that the director and crew were born in period of peace following the Second World War and therefore have no affinity with protagonists who burn with a sense of mission, the same that do it all "for the sake of mankind!" or "to protect the earth!"

Shinji is decisively different from lead characters in other robot animation series. His motivation in continuing his tough mission as an Eva pilot is the selfish desire to have his father "recognize his abilities."

Ever since he was a child, Shinji has felt unloved by his father, or that he wasn't really

See Glossary
Shinji Ikari
Pilot
Evangelion

wanted. He becomes an Eva pilot because it enables him to feel "he is needed" by his father.

Such psychological characterizations appear throughout the Evangelion story. Anno probably judged that his lead character would provoke more sympathy from his audience if he infused him with self-doubt and selfish desires that most people could relate to.

Part of the success of Evangelion is the relationship that Shinji manages to create with the viewers.

See questions
1 5 15 45

Whose cells are used to clone Rei Ayanami? 25

In the middle of the Evangelion series we find out that Rei Ayanami, the First Children, is a clone, though we never find out whose cells were used in the cloning. We can, however, get close to unraveling this mystery by piecing together events from different episodes and from what some of the characters say.

Firstly there is the overly careful manner in which Gendo treats Rei, and how Rei reciprocates with an affection that borders on love. To add to this, in Episode 15 Shinji looks at Rei, who is ringing out some wet clothes, and says, "I feel like I'm looking at my mother when I look at you Ayanami."

In Episode 5, Rei asks Shinji, "Don't you believe your own father?" to which Shinji replies, "Well, it stands to reason, don't it. A guy like him!" For his troubles he gets a slap in the face from Rei in very much the same way a mother would react to a selfish child.

On top of that, in Episode 14, the first

See Glossary
Rei Ayanami
Gendo Ikari
Shinji Ikari

episode to establish compatibility between machine and pilot, Rei slips into the cockpit of Eva-01 and Shinji into Eva-00, and it becomes clear that their personal patterns are extremely similar.

Based on the events in this particular episode, it's not too much of a leap of faith to believe that the cells used to clone Rei came from Yui Ikari - Shinji's mother.

Yui is cited as having come to an unfortunate end during experiments conducted at the No. 2 Lab deep in the earth below Hakone in the year 2004. Still, there's a lot about the incident that remains unclear. Indeed, Dr Naoko Akagi says little more than, "She disappeared in the midst of conducting an irregular experiment."

However, in Episode 24 Shinji himself is absorbed into the entry plug. From what Ritsuko Akagi remarks - "That was something we tried and failed ten years ago." - we can surmise that Yui was also absorbed into the workings of the cockpit.

When we recall that it was Yui's DNA that was recovered from the entry plug, it's a small step to believing that the same DNA was used to clone Rei. However, as we know today that a cloned entity has no received memories from its DNA donor, the question remains as to

See Glossary
Pilot
Yui Ikari
Naoko Akagi
Ritsuko Akagi
Entry Plug

why Rei functions according to the memories of Yui.

In Episode 23 Rei initially self-destructs while trying to save Shinji, and a new, third Rei appears, though she does not appear to have quite the same personality of the previous Rei. In fact, in the same Episode 23 there is a scene showing a number of Reis floating in a tank filled with LCL deep in the bowels of Central Dogma. Ritsuko Akagi explains, "Rei was the only receptacle capable of housing a soul. She was the only one without a soul."

All this suggests that Rei is not a mere clone, but a receptacle with a soul, and that soul most likely came from Yui. That's why Rei feels affection for Gendo and maternal feelings toward Shinji.

We also get some insight into the relationship between Rei and the Evas. From the lines, "Evas, born of Adam," it is evident that the Evas were made based on Adam.

Does it then follow that humans made robots based on the image of Adam?

Probably not. It is more likely that the Evas were created with both the cloned cells of Adam and the souls of human beings, beginning with Yui, at their core. Rei is a clone, and at the same time a receptacle for a soul.

See Glossary
LCL
Central Dogma
Evangelion
Adam
Core

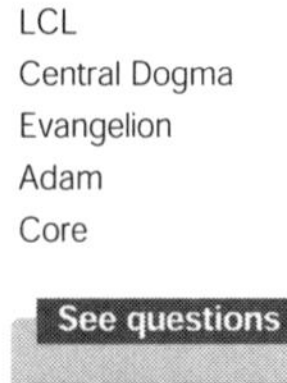

EVA Profile 009

Name **Gendo Ikari**

Commander in Chief of NERV.
Age: 48
NERV ID: Unknown
Date of Birth: April 29, 1967
Blood type: A
Talents: Information manipulation
Interests: Insidious plots, secrets

It is impossible to oppose Gendo in his lair at NERV, as he is the possessor of absolute power. Extremely charismatic, with numerous capable staff reporting to him, he likes to play hardball and will stop at nothing to achieve his ends. It follows that Gendo is extremely cold-blooded and cruel, illustrated in his actions in doing absolutely nothing for his son for three full years. He is often away from NERV on official business. Having said which, he has strong feelings for his late wife Yui Ikari.

Gendo is responsible not only for the fight against the Angels, but also the Human Completion Project. He is also noted for continually readjusting his spectacles on his nose.

碇
ゲンドウ

Why does Asuka have such mental problems? 26

Besides Shinji, who's father forces him to pilot an Eva, and Rei, who goes about her job uncomplainingly, Asuka is the only one who is openly proud of her role as a pilot, and who undertakes her tasks with enthusiasm.

Proud and a sore loser, Asuka has a strong independent streak. She is so astounded to discover that Shinji is the better pilot that she loses all confidence, her synchro-ratio slumps, and she has a nervous breakdown following an attack from the 15th Angel.

It appears that Asuka's mother also suffers from mental problems, and even attempts to kill herself and her child. She finally succeeds in suicide, hanging herself in hospital the very same day that Asuka is designated as Second Children. In Episode 22 we are told that her problems are set off "as the result of contact experiments."

These tests are most likely connected with the Evas, and we can surmise that her

See Glossary
Shinji Ikari
Pilot
Evangelion
Rei Ayanami
Asuka Langley Soryu
Synchro-Ratio
Angel
Kyoko Langley Soryu

psychological state is the result of her soul being absorbed by the core of Eva-02.

In Asuka's case it is clear that she is tormented by loneliness due to her relationship with her stepmother after her father remarries. This explains why she decides to "be strong, and live dependent on no one else."

Being an Eva pilot must have been one of her key mental supports. That leads us to believe that although her reasons are somewhat different to those of Shinji, Asuka's motives for becoming an Eva pilot are also self-motivated.

To suddenly realize that there is a superior pilot to her and that she can no longer synchronize with the Eva must be an enormous blow to her confidence. This is what obviously leads to her eventual breakdown.

See Glossary
Core

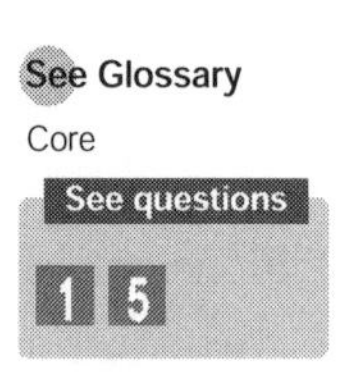

Is Misato Katsuragi really a top warrior, or just a slob? 27

Misato Katsuragi is the head of Military Operations at NERV, directing the Evas in their fight against the encroaching Angels. But while playing this successful, professional role, she also comes across as someone who prefers getting drunk and enjoying the moment rather than thinking of tomorrow. The maternal affection that she has for Shinji is yet another facet of her personality.

Misato is a fierce freedom fighter, a slob and a big sister all rolled into one. She might just be the most elaborately described character in Evangelion.

In the year 2000 she accompanies her father - Dr Katsuragi - and his research unit on a trip to Antarctica, where she walks smack into the Second Impact. Her father places her in an escape capsule, allowing her to flee with her life. She later joins the organization that would become NERV to fight the Angels. Although she has grown to hate her father, she holds the Angels responsible for his death.

See Glossary
Misato Katsuragi
NERV
Evangelion
Angel
Shinji Ikari
Dr Katsuragi
Antarctica
Second Impact

It is later revealed that she suffered aphasia, the inability to speak, following the Second Impact, and spent two silent years in a mental hospital. That seems to provide enough of a reason for her to devote herself to the destruction of the Angels.

Although she has grown to hate her father, she appears to harbor something of a father complex. The reason she splits up with her lover Ryoji Kaji is because, "I realized I had started to see elements of my father in him."

While this complex may appear to weigh heavily on her, darkening the mood of her character, she is also something of a rebel who can happily start the day on toast and two beers. She lives in an apartment that looks like a garbage tip and manages to mangle the directions on instant food packages - and even canned food - making her a disaster in the kitchen.

There is a secret to the make-up of Misato's character. The storyboards editor once asked Hideaki Anno what kind of person Misato is. Anno reportedly replied, "Like Tsuki no Usagi of Sailor Moon."

See Glossary
Ryoji Kaji

In *Sailor Moon* the 14-year-old Tsuki no Usagi eventually morphs into the heroine Sailor Moon to fight evil. But Tsuki no Usagi is also known as a bit of a doofus.

Who killed Ryoji Kaji? 28

Ryoji Kaji is officially the head of the Special Surveillance Department at NERV, which he joined after returning from the German satellite office with Asuka.

However, at the entrance to Central Dogma, Misato sticks a gun in his back saying, "Well, well, well, if it isn't Ryoji Kaji of the Japanese government's surveillance unit." Kaji has little choice but to come clean. "Was it that obvious?" he asks.

Kaji meets up with Japanese government agents on numerous occasions, and each time the conversation touches on confidential information. Kaji is a Japanese government spy who has infiltrated NERV.

He also passes on Japanese government intelligence about the Jet Alone Project to NERV, making him a double agent. The Japanese government knows nothing of this, but Gendo has him figured out and chooses to let him remain at large.

Kaji's true character is revealed in Episode

See Glossary
Ryoji Kaji
NERV
Asuka Langley Soryu
Central Dogma
Misato Katsuragi
Jet Alone
Gendo Ikari

21, when we find out that he is really a member of SEELE. It is SEELE that has sent in Kaji to monitor Gendo. But in the same episode Kaji gets killed...and we're not told by whom. As he works for NERV, SEELE and the Japanese government, his killer could be anyone.

Also in Episode 21 Kaji chooses to free Fuyutsuki, who has been kidnapped by SEELE. He then writes out his will and sends it to Misato. He also leaves a message on her answering machine.

His last words are, "Well, you took your time, didn't you?" It's clear he's talking to his assassin. Based on the little we know, his killer was most likely sent by SEELE.

Why does Fuyutsuki cooperate with Gendo? 29

Kozo Fuyutsuki is a man of mystery. We find out much of what we know about him in Episode 21, when he tells us he once taught at Kyoto University, where he ran the Department of Science's No. 1 Lab and was a successful professor of metabiology. It was there that he met Yui Ikari, who had submitted a thought-provoking report on bioengineering.

Fuyutsuki first meets Gendo at the Kyoto Prefectural Police HQ. It is 1999. Gendo, who gets to "go down the station," after getting into a drunken fight, nominates Fuyutsuki as his guarantor...despite never having met him. According to Gendo, he has heard about Fuyutsuki from Yui Ikari and is drawn to his character.

When Fuyutsuki turns up and judges Gendo to be, "Crummier than I'd thought," Gendo conjures up a smile that doesn't really suit him and tells Fuyutsuki, "You, Professor, are everything I envisaged." It appears that Gendo

See Glossary
Kozo Fuyutsuki
Yui Ikari
Gendo Ikari

has made a point of getting close to Fuyutsuki as he has great hopes for his own plans for humanity. Fuyutsuki is 40 years old and Gendo 32 when all this takes place.

There is a telling episode that reveals Gendo's all-important plans for humanity. It is an exchange between Fuyutsuki and Gendo that takes place at the Artificial Evolution Laboratory in Hakone.

Sensing that the real cause of the Second Impact has been whitewashed by the UN, Fuyutsuki begins to smell a rat. In his own investigation, made from a deep sense of moral outrage, he begins to get close to the truth, and thrusts his findings under the nose of Gendo, who is in cahoots with SEELE.

In an act of defiance, Fuyutsuki says, "I have no intention of letting those responsible for the Second Impact just walk away. I will reveal the existence of SEELE, and the contents of the Dead Sea Scrolls."

Later, however, Gendo leads Fuyutsuki down to GeoFront far below Hakone, and reveals to him the Evangelion development project. Gendo makes Fuyutsuki a proposal, "Won't you come and work with me creating a new history for mankind?" Fuyutsuki is won over, and his mindset changes 180 degrees.

One year later, Fuyutsuki, who was once

See Glossary
Second Impact
SEELE
Secret Dead Sea Scrolls
GeoFront
Evangelion

adamantly opposed to SEELE, is in with the organization up to his neck. When he berates Gendo for going missing for a week in the wake of the disappearance of Yui Ikari in 2004, we clearly see that he has chosen to throw all his weight behind the SEELE-initiated Human Completion Plan.

We are left wondering what it is that has led to such a transformation.

One possibility is that there is something in the SEELE Human Completion Plan that pricked his sense of justice. Conversely, maybe from the very start Gendo has figured out that there is something in the justification for the Human Completion Plan that is strong enough to appeal to even Fuyutsuki, and it is that which makes him approach the professor in the first place.

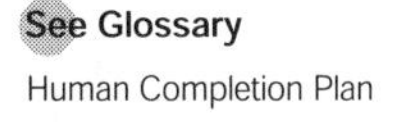
See Glossary
Human Completion Plan

EVA Profile 010

Name **Kozo Fuyutsuki**

冬月コウゾウ

Sub-commander of NERV.
Age: 60+
NERV ID: Unknown
Date of Birth: April 9
Blood type: AB
Talents: Talent spotting
Interests: Chess problems

Kozo has been friends with Gendo since his university days and is always by his side when working. He serves as an effective commander when Gendo is absent. A very low-key and laid-back kind of person with clear powers of judgment, Kozo almost never loses his cool. It is unclear why he accepted Gendo's offer to join NERV.

Does Ritsuko Akagi really love Gendo? 36

Ritsuko Akagi is the systems administrator of the MAGI, the mother computer at the heart of NERV. She's also involved in researching and analyzing vast amounts of data related to the Evas.

However, she is also having an affair with her boss Gendo. And this is not the kind of affair where the talented woman is a fool when it comes to love. The relationship between the two reveals the complicated nature of Ritsuko's personality.

Ritsuko's mother, the scientist Naoko Akagi, was also once Gendo's lover, and we find out from the story that Ritsuko is aware of this all along. This leaves us wondering what kind of person she is that she becomes the lover of her mother's ex.

Naoko Akagi was an accomplished scientist. So much so, we can imagine, that she gave everything to her work and neglected her child. Ritsuko is fated to be forever compared to her mother after she chooses to follow in her foot-

See Glossary
Ritsuko Akagi
MAGI System
NERV
Evangelion
Gendo Ikari
Naoko Akagi

steps and become a scientist.

She must have been driven by the need to surpass her mother, who was immersed in her research. It would not be unusual for someone such as Ritsuko to harbor a certain hatred for her mother. She may well believe she is going one better than her mother when she is making love to Gendo.

But Ritsuko's feelings start coming apart at the seams. She tells Gendo, "I never once enjoyed our love-making." She kills the clones of Rei Ayanami that Gendo has so carefully nurtured in tanks. Many fans may interpret such words and actions to mean that Ritsuko wasn't really in love with Gendo, but slept with him out of a sense of rivalry with her mother.

But we have to wonder if that isn't putting the cart before the horse. It may have been rivalry that first induced her to sleep with Gendo. But there are indications that she really grows to love him.

However, she is unable to control her emotions, and says things to Gendo she neither feels nor means. The same is true when she destroys the clones in a jealous tantrum.

There are many complex characters in Evangelion, and Ritsuko is definitely one of them.

See Glossary
Rei Ayanami

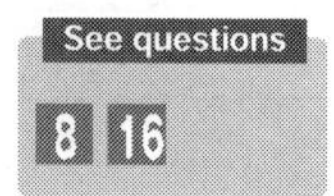

What is Gendo's real reason for promoting the Human Completion Plan? 31

Gendo Ikari is the supreme commander of NERV. As the story unfolds, however, we find out that he is not simply a cog in the machine but has a burning ambition all of his own, and that he may well be using NERV merely as a way to achieve it. It's quite clear that this ambition is the implementation of the Human Completion Plan.

The question is, why?

We know that Gendo is not driven by a sense of justice like Fuyutsuki. After all, he has his son take on the dangerous role of Eva pilot. In the event of any failure to capture the eighth Angel when Asuka dives into the active Mt. Asama volcanic crater, Gendo has a fully loaded bomber circling the mountain on stand-by, and is quite prepared to sacrifice everyone including Ritsuko and Misato.

Gendo is selfish and without pity - it is impossible to imagine him doing something for the sake of mankind. His reasons for pursuing the Human Completion Plan must be personal

See Glossary
Gendo Ikari
NERV
Human Completion Plan
Kozo Fuyutsuki
Shinji Ikari
Evangelion
Pilot
Angel
Asuka Langley Soryu
Mount Asama
Ritsuko Akagi
Misato Katsuragi

in nature.

We will touch on the differences between the SEELE and Gendo Human Completion Plans in Q34. But just to give you a hint - it's all tied up with Yui, the woman he loved.

See Glossary
SEELE
Yui Ikari

See questions
4 6 8 17
34 35 36

Why were few Evangelion toys initially made? 32

Evangelion is not your average robot anime. As such, there is less focus on detailing the mechanics used in the story.This may have been influenced by its association with *Devilman*, but there is at least one other important reason.

At the planning stage, director Hideaki Anno is reported to have said, "With recent robot anime series there have been too many instances of toy makers sticking their big noses in from the design stage so they can get a spec that is easy to turn into a toy. I don't want any interference from toy makers, so I'm going to design a robot that just cannot be turned into a toy."

This anecdote reveals Anno's rebellious streak. He is known for his disdain of the cozy relationship between animation creators and toy makers.

Then we come to the design.

When the character designer Yoshiyuki Sadamoto met with Anno to discuss the design of Rei Ayanami, the director told him, "Whatever

See Glossary
Evangelion
Rei Ayanami

else, she needs to be painted in as a bitterly unhappy young girl with little sense of presence."

That put Sadamoto in mind to create a character lying in bed covered in bandages.

This is why Rei Ayanami first appears before Shinji with one eye covered in a gauze and the other half of her face and her entire body in bandages. She is not injured. It was simply necessary from a design point of view to have her bandaged up. Any implied injuries in the storyline are subservient to design concerns.

Arguably, it is because of Anno's dictates on design that few Evangelion toys were initially made. But figures of Rei, in all her bandaged beauty, sold like wild fire. This is probably the first and only example of an animated series where reproductions of the human characters outsold those of the robots.

See Glossary
Shinji Ikari

Neon Genesis Evangelion
The Core

Cosplay Model: Takeshi Goda

How are Evangelion and the Old Testament connected? 33

Legends from Christianity and Judaism are utilized in the storyline throughout Evangelion, beginning with the story of Adam and Eve and the Fruit of Knowledge. Other important religious mechanisms are sprinkled throughout, such as the Spear of Longinus and the Tree of Life.

To really appreciate the story, it is important to grasp some of the terminology and techniques.

* It says in the Book of Genesis, "So God created man in his own image, in the image of God created he him; male and female created he them." It also says, "And Adam called his wife's name Eve; because she was the mother of all living." This is where the story of Evangelion begins. This is also underscored by the words of Naoko in Episode 21, "That which is made in the image of Adam - Eve."

* It is recorded in the Book of Genesis that, "And when the woman saw that the tree was good for food,

See Glossary
Adam
Fruit of Knowledge
Spear of Longinus
Tree of Life
Naoko Akagi
Evangelion

and that it was pleasant to the eyes, and a tree to be desired to make one wise, she took of the fruit thereof, and did eat, and gave also unto her husband with her; and he did eat." This is the essence of Original Sin. In Episode 12, while looking at Antarctica in the wake of the Second Impact, Gendo says, "This is a world cleansed of the blemish of Original Sin."

* It is also recorded in the Book of Genesis that, "And the eyes of both of them were opened, and they knew they were naked; and they sewed fig leaves together, and made themselves aprons." In Episode 17, Gendo says, "That weakest of living creatures built himself a paradise for mankind with the knowledge he acquired because of his very weakness."

* It is further recorded in the Book of Genesis that, "And the Lord God said, 'Behold, the man is become as one of us, to know good and evil: and now, lest he put forth his hand, and take also of the Tree of Life, and eat, and live forever.' Therefore the Lord God sent him forth from the Garden of Eden, to till the ground from whence he was taken." In Episode 17, Gendo says, "There was nothing for Mankind to do; expelled from the Garden of Eden, he was left to escape to the earth to live cheek and jowl with death."

See Glossary
Antarctica
Second Impact
Gendo Ikari

* It says in the Book of Genesis, "And the Lord God said, Behold, the man is become as one of us, to know

good and evil: and now, lest he put forth his hand, and take also of the Tree of Life, and eat, and live for ever:" In Episode 26, Fuyutsuki says, "The Fruit of Life born by the Angels, and the Fruit of Knowledge born by human beings. Eva-01 has acquired both of these gifts, and so has become something to rival the power of God."

* It is recorded in the Book of Genesis that, "So he drove out the man; and he placed at the east of the Garden of Eden Cherubim, and a flaming sword which turned every way, to keep the way of the Tree of Life." In Episode 11, Rei Ayanami says, "Man was afraid of the darkness, and used light to extinguish the darkness and live." Asuka's reaction is, "Baby, that there is pheelosopheeee!!" Shinji chimes in, "So I guess that makes human beings special? Maybe that is why the Angels are attacking?"

See Glossary
Kozo Fuyutsuki
Fruit of Life
Angel
Humans
Rei Ayanami
Asuka Langley Soryu
Shinji Ikari

See questions
34 35 36 37
38 39 40 41
42 43 44 45

As we can see, it is no exaggeration to say that Evangelion is based on the Old Testament.

EVA Profile 011

Name **Ryoji Kaji**

Head of the Special Surveillance Department of NERV.
Age: 30
NERV ID: Unknown
Date of Birth: June 17, 1984
Blood type: A
Talents: Spying
Interests: Growing watermelons

Ryoji is posted to NERV HQ after returning to Japan from Germany along with Asuka and Eva-02. Aloof and something of a tough guy, Ryoji is in fact a triple agent - working for NERV, SEELE and the Japanese government. Normally mild, if prone to lead with the lip, he can be very serious when the occasion calls for it. He shacked up with Misato at university, and he tries to win her back. But all the while, it is Asuka who has secret feelings for him. He is finally bumped off as "the man who knew too much."

加持
リョウジ

What is the difference between the Gendo and SEELE Human Completion Plans? 34

As was stated in Q33, the basic viewpoint of Evangelion is cosmic: human beings are burdened with Original Sin. The question is - How can human beings be released from this?

Plan 1: Release through penance for eating the Fruit of Knowledge, returning to a happier time when everything was one.

This is the SEELE proposal, as can be seen from the lines in Episode 26, "We will bring happiness to human beings in its true form."

Plan 2: Exploit the Fruit of Knowledge - science - to the ultimate degree, using all the capabilities of human beings themselves to artificially remedy inadequacies, and continue living, even as a new life-form. Final analysis: to acquire the Fruit of Life, and by doing so move closer to God.

This is Gendo's plan as indicated from what he says in Episode 25, "Humans should push ever onward toward a new world. That is what the Eva series is all about." Also, from the

See Glossary
Fruit of Knowledge
SEELE
Fruit of Life
Gendo Ikari
Evangelion

words of Keel Lorentz in Episode 24, "But it seems there is a man who is attempting to acquire powers close to those of a God."

Lets quickly go over the ways in which Gendo and SEELE hope to achieve their aims, and point to a number of scenes that underscore those approaches.

SEELE Plan: Attempting to free humans from Original Sin and return them to the Garden of Eden. According to the Life of Christ, Jesus, the Son of God, was executed by being crucified on a cross made from the Tree of Life, and the blood that flowed onto the earth cleansed the sins of man in a ritual of penance.

* In Episode 26, Keel says, "Now is the time to resurrect the central tree."
* and, "We have recovered the original Spear of Longinus."
* and finally, "Let the ritual begin."

In order to put this plan into action, the first thing that is necessary is the Tree of Life. Next, the Spear of Longinus is needed to kill Christ on the cross. To follow the Son of God, twelve disciples, or Angels are required. And when the Son of God, who is to be crucified, is added, we arrive at the number 13.

If man is freed from Original Sin as

See Glossary
Keel Lorentz
Spear of Longinus
Tree of Life

planned, he will revert to a stage prior to that when he was forced to assume the burden of Original Sin, with the roots of life equating to the Egg of Lilith. This can be found in Keel's words in Episode 26: "We both start and end in the same place. Good. Let us begin."

Gendo Plan: Gendo is looking to acquire a power close to that of God by first producing the Tree of Life, acquiring the Fruit of Life, then combining this with the Fruit of Knowledge.

In other words, the Gendo plan aims for man not to regress to a primitive stage, but to evolve to the next stage.

* In Episode 21, Gendo says, "This is the way to God that no one has ever achieved."
* In Episode 26, Fuyutsuki says," The Fruit of Life borne by the Angels, and the Fruit of Knowledge borne by human beings. Eva-01 has acquired both of these gifts, and so has become something to rival the power of God."

See Glossary
Angel
Egg of Lilith
Yui Ikari
Rei Ayanami

Human beings are also Angels, and in the final analysis it is the humans that are the problem. So, if everything goes according to plan, human beings will survive as an entity with powers close to those of God, once they have defeated the Angels, producing the Tree of Life and having Gendo fuse with the Eva - Yui - via the medium of Rei.

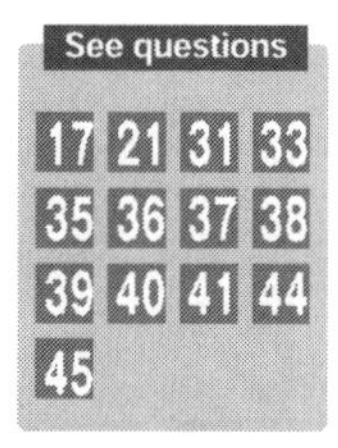

See questions
17 21 31 33
35 36 37 38
39 40 41 44
45

EVA Profile 012

Name **Maya Ibuki**

Second Lieutenant in the Technology Department at NERV
Age: 24
NERV ID: Unknown
Date of Birth: July 11, 1984
Blood type: A
Talents: Computers
Interests: Programming, reading

Maya reports to Ritsuko Akagi. She works on the floor of NERV HQ, monitoring the Eva pilots. She is perhaps the most "normal" of any of the characters appearing in Evangelion. She even has a pink cushion on her office chair.

伊吹マヤ

Do Gendo and SEELE clash over their differing Human Completion Plans? 35

As we have seen, both Gendo and SEELE are pursuing Human Completion Plans. But the two plans lead them off in two entirely different directions.

The common element to both plans is arguably the Tree of Life.

The process of the Tree of Life is detailed in the Dead Sea Scrolls. It is necessary to defeat the Angels that defend the Tree of Life, as detailed in the Old Testament. Therefore, although the end result may differ, there are points on which Gendo and SEELE can cooperate.

1. Interpretation of the Dead Sea Scrolls

Makes it possible to understand the mechanism of the emergence of the Angels and the Tree of Life, making the discovery of the Spear of Longinus vital. This we can tell from the following scenes and lines:

SEELE - "We have finally defeated the 16th Angel."
SEELE - "That leaves just one of the Angels listed

See Glossary
Gendo Ikari
SEELE
Human Completion Plan
Tree of Life
Dead Sea Scrolls
Angel
Spear of Longinus

in the SEELE Dead Sea scrolls".
SEELE - "The promised time is drawing close."

2. Second Impact

The Spear of Longinus to be used to have Adam - the source of the Angels - revert to an egg before attempting to destroy the Angels.

However, the fusion with human DNA, which is a condition for having Adam revert to an egg, sets off an anti-AT Field that exceeds expectations - as the fusion of the Fruit of Knowledge and the Fruit of Life result in the power of God. As a result, Adam is blown up by a link to explosives set in place to cope with unforeseen eventualities. Kaoru Nagisa, who was born on the same day as the Second Impact, becomes the final Angel.

3. The Adam Plan and the E-Plan

These plans are vital to both the destruction of the Angels and the Human Completion Plan - the ritual of penance. At first these plans were one, but they later split.

The Adam Plan
The plan to revitalize the original Adam. While also being used to create the Evangelions - the E-Plan - SEELE plans to use the original Adam in its ritual of penance. However, Gendo seizes on the

See Glossary
Second Impact
Adam
Anti-AT Field
Kaoru Nagisa
Adam Regeneration Plan
E-Plan
Evangelion
Fruit of Knowledge
Fruit of Life

idea for use in his own Human Completion Plan.

The E-Plan

The project to produce the 12 Evangelions to perform the rituals as well as destroy the Angels. Lilith is used until the Adam Regeneration Plan gets under way. However, after the Adam Regeneration Plan is operational with the emergence of Eva-02, the Evas are produced using Adam himself.

4. The Destruction of the Angels

This is a condition for the emergence of the Tree of Life, and is achieved by the use of Eva-01 (Episodes 1 - 24). Essential for both the SEELE plan, which will use the original Adam in its ritual of penance, and the Gendo plan, for which to acquire the Fruit of Life.

However, this is a necessary process for both plans, and that is why SEELE and Gendo cooperate to kill off the Angels one by one while keeping each other in check - with the Spear of Longinus, the S2 Organ and the NERV anti-personnel defense system - as they retain in their sights the Tree of Life.

See Glossary
Lilith
S2 Organ

EVA Profile 013

Name Yui Ikari

Deceased
Date of Birth: March 30, 1977
Blood type: O
Talents: Unknown
Interests: Mountain climbing

碇
ユイ

Apart from the fact that she is Shinji's mother, we know little about Yui as she appears only a few times before being killed off. She leaves many mysteries behind, including why she ever married Gendo. She has a special connection with Eva- 01.

Name Naoko Akagi

Deceased
Date of Birth: Unknown
Blood type: Unknown
Talents: Developing computer systems

赤木
ナオコ

Naoko was the developer of the MAGI system and hence originator of the Evas. An extremely capable scientist, she was eventually driven to suicide after an affair with Gendo. Before doing so however, she implanted her three contradictory personalities into the MAGI system.

How does all this talk of Gendo's plan and SEELE's plan actually turn out? 36

From the moment that the last Angel - Kaoru Nagisa - is destroyed, Gendo and SEELE revert to being enemies, becoming embroiled in a battle over the Tree of Life.

SEELE had originally wanted to exclude pilots from the Evas. Thanks to Misato, however, it could not prevent Shinji - "the child of God" in one reading of his name - from piloting the Eva-01. The Eva is executed with the Spear of Longinus on the crucifix of the Tree of Life while Shinji is still in the entry plug.

At the same time, Shinji's Eva, having managed to reach the Tree of Life, becomes a god with the power to decide the future. Rei - read as "spirit" - is then awakened to her role as the mother of God - Lilith - by Shinji's cries of fear and loneliness. Gendo's plan is thwarted as Rei refuses to fuse with her father, Gendo, forcing all the power of life to revert to the womb.

As a consequence, the SEELE plan of having mankind freed from Original Sin is

See Glossary

Angel
Kaoru Nagisa
Gendo Ikari
SEELE
Tree of Life
Pilot
Misato Katsuragi
Shinji Ikari
Evangelion
Spear of Longinus
Rei Ayanami
Lilith
Entry Plug

achieved and the barrier - the AT Field - between human beings that has existed since Man first ate of the Fruit of Knowledge is removed. Humans begin to fuse, reverting to the source of life - the Egg of Lilith, or the Black Moon.

It is now that Gendo realizes Yui does exist. But after telling her of his true feelings for her, he conjures up an image of her being swallowed up by Shinji's Eva. This is an expression of his desire to tell Shinji of his sorrow and fear, but more than anything else, it is an illustration of his feelings as a father in wanting to fuse with Shinji and not Yui.

Shinji has been in a catatonic state since killing Kaoru, but after much worry decides against fusion, choosing instead co-existence with other beings, who kill and hurt each other. He chooses to be born from the womb of Lilith - along with Asuka - and go out into the real world and live among mankind, to whom all are strangers.

So, he decides to cut his links with both Yui - who fused with the Eva - and Lilith - the mother of mankind - and says goodbye to his mother. Both mothers recognize that decision, choosing their own destruction in order to allow Shinji to become an independent human being.

See Glossary
AT Field
Fruit of Knowledge
Egg of Lilith
Black Moon
Yui Ikari
Asuka Langley Soryu

In closing, let's mention something about Asuka. She says, "I will never have children," based on her experience of seeing her mother go insane and eventually commit suicide after being abandoned by her father, who took off with another woman. She chooses not to become a mother, even while maintaining affection for her own mother due to the complexes born of her mother's tragedy.

In other words, she turns her back on her own maternal feelings. But, at the very least, she manages to recover her trust for her mother when she sits in the cockpit of Eva-02. Then there is a final symbolic scene: Asuka appears as Rei - the mother of mankind Lilith - with all her bandages and eye-pads. Of course, this scene is meant to show that Asuka has mended her heart and reawakened to her maternal side. This is when she becomes Eve - the mother of a new species of human beings in a new era.

See Glossary
Kyoko Langley Soryu
See questions
17 31 34 35
37 38 39 40
41 42 43 44
45

EVA Profile 014

Name Evangelion-01

エヴァンゲリオン 初号機

"The multipurpose android weapon," that NERV spent 14 years creating with funds from the national budget to fight the Angels. The craft developed are known in NERV as Eva. While developed at locations around the world, only three craft are in full working service. The first to go into battle is Eva-01 piloted by Shinji. The Evas operate via a cable electric supply.

Name Evangelion-00

The Eva piloted by First Children, Rei Ayanami. It is known as a prototype. The craft runs amok after activation tests fail, and it is rendered inoperable via a Bakelite freezing process. In very basic terms, only the head and shoulder portions are different to Eva-01. There is no marked difference in performance characteristics. Its coloring - orange-tinted yellow - takes something from the practice craft used by the Japanese Imperial Navy. It is revised from Episode 11 and becomes blue.

Name Evangelion-02

エヴァンゲリオン 弐号機

The Eva piloted by Asuka Langley Soryu, chosen as Second Children. The third craft to be produced, it becomes the standard model. The design and parts are manufactured in Japan, with assembly and activation tests conducted in Germany. The craft is painted crimson red, and its external features include a head portion mounted with four supplementary optical sensors. It is armed with a Progressive Knife. NERV refers to the model armed with the knife as simply "B-type equipment." It appears from Episode 8, where the prodigy Asuka controls the craft at will.

What is the relationship between Adam and the Second Impact? 37

In the Old Testament, Adam is the first man, created by God. Eve was created from Adam's rib. What this tells us is that Adam, the first human being, was hermaphrodite, capable of reproducing. In the Kabbalah, Adam is listed as capable of giving birth to all things, while at the same time being the entity to which all things revert.

At the time of the Second Impact, the scientists name the giant that emerges Adam. Naoko says of the Giant of Light, "In GEHIRN, we call that Giant of Light Adam." In simple terms, Adam is equated with the Giant of Light.

But what exactly happened at the Second Impact?

From the opening scene of the anime movie, *Death and Rebirth,* we know that human DNA is fused with the first Angel. That is conducted using the Spear of Longinus and compressing the donor DNA into the Giant of Light. This is what sets off the Second Impact. In other words, the Second Impact is the

See Glossary
Adam
Evangelion
Kabbalah
Naoko Akagi
Giant of Light
GEHIRN
Angel
Spear of Longinus
Second Impact

fusion of humans and Angels.

There are two stages to this process. The first is the giant that was discovered, and the second is the fusion of the Giant of Light with human DNA. Both of these stages involve the same life form, though this is split into two in the strictest terms.

"First Angel" refers to the first stage. We know from *Death and Rebirth* that there is a period of time between the discovery of the giant and the experimental fusion with the human DNA that sets off the Second Impact. During this time, a large number of experiments are carried out using the first Angel.

Ritsuko says, "The humans had stumbled upon God, so they made the most of it and tried to own him. That's why they were cursed. That was 15 years ago, and the God they stumbled upon has disappeared. But now they're trying to resurrect God on their own. That's Adam, and they're trying to make a being in the image of God from Adam. That's Eve."

The feeding of the human DNA through the Spear of Longinus resulted in the Giant of Light being able to walk, but also set off the Second Impact. The Bakelite Adam was reconstituted using the fragments from the explosion, and Eva-02 was constructed from this.

See Glossary
Bakelite

In other words, there are two meanings to the term - Adam.

1. The primitive Adam - the First Angel

As we can understand from Kaoru's words, "Adam. The mother of all existence. Must all that is born of Adam revert to Adam?" Adam has given birth to all life forms from his own body. This also appears in the Old Testament. In the Kabbalah, Adam is described as the beginning of all things, and the being to which all must revert. In other words, God.

2. The Giant of Light, Adam. (Adam fused with human DNA)

As we can understand from what Gendo says, "That's it. Adam the first human being." Adam is the first of a new race of humans.

See Glossary
Kaoru Nagisa
Gendo Ikari

See questions
6 9 10 11
21 33

EVA File 001

What's in a Name

There are a many fascinating characters in Evangelion, not the least Rei Ayanami, Ritsuko Akagi and Maya Ibuki. However, few fans are aware of the origins of their names. Interestingly, some of the lead characters have been named after ships of the now-defunct Japanese Imperial Navy, which were obviously chosen by Anno because of their own interesting histories.

Character	Type of Vessel	Vessel's Name
Ritsuko Akagi	Aircraft Carrier	Akagi
Misato Katsuragi	Aircraft Carrier	Katsuragi
Asuka Langley Soryu	Aircraft Carrier	Soryu
Maya Ibuki	Aircraft Carrier	Ibuki
Rei Ayanami	Destroyer	Ayanami
Kozo Fuyutsuki	Super Destroyer	Fuyutsuki

Akagi

Following the London Disarmament Treaty, Japan's unfinished battle cruiser was remodeled to be Japan's No. 2 aircraft carrier. By the time it participated in the Pacific theater of operations during WWII, it was already an old vessel. However, at the time it was built, the Akagi was recognized as the largest and strongest ship of its class in the world. It sank at the Battle of Midway.

Katsuragi

Built during a period of increased production immediately preceding the outbreak of the Pacific War, the Katsuragi was a remodeled version of the Hiryu class aircraft carriers. Altogether five were planned, only three were completed by the end of the war, the third of which never saw battle, but was used as a transport ship before being dismantled.

Soryu

The Soryu was a midsize aircraft carrier of original design. One of the most famous WWII vessels in the Imperial Navy, it was sunk at the Battle of Midway.

Ibuki

Remodeled while under construction but never completed, the Ibuki was dismantled after WWII.

Ayanami

One of 10 versions of the remodeled Fubuki class destroyer, the Ayanami was revolutionary at the time. By the outbreak of WWII, it had become the standard for Japanese destroyers. The Ayanami sank during the Guadalcanal Campaign.

Many of the names of the characters in Evangelion have meanings that are not clearly apparent.

Shinji means Child of God, Rei means Spirit and Gendo means, literally, "speech and conduct." This is taken from the lines of the New Testament, "In the beginning, there was the Word, and the Word was with God, and the Word was God."

If we accept that the father is God, Shinji is the Son of God and Rei is the spirit, we arrive at the Father, the Son and the Holy Spirit - the Holy Trinity that is the key Catholic dogma.

"Mass" in Japanese is "misa," and therefore, Misato is "one who presides over Mass." This is reinforced by her black blouse and the crucifix she always wears. "Ritsuko" derives from "rippo," one meaning of which is "Rule of God," a doctrine of Judaism. However, in this case it means that, with the MAGI system, she supports the "Son of God," Shinji. She somewhat resembles pop singer Madonna, suggesting Mary, the mother of Christ.

The names of Shinji's classmates, Kensuke Aida and Toji Suzuhara, are both taken from the Ryu Murakami novel *Fascism in Love and Fantasy* (Ai to Genso no Fascism).

EVA File 002

Movies and Events

On March 15, 1997, Neon Genesis Evangelion: Death and Rebirth hit the big screen. Fans crowded Tokyo theaters, with people lining for hundreds of yards. An estimated 150,000 people saw the movie on its opening day, and box-office takings hit a record 200 million yen ($2 million). The 40,000 limited edition tickets that came with an Eva telephone card sold out in advance in a matter of hours, and advance tickets sales overall were within the 200,000 mark. Until then, the record for an anime movie had been held by Adieu Galaxy Express 999, which opened at theaters in 1979 with advance tickets sales of 160,000.

1,300 fans applied for tickets to the advance preview of Death and Rebirth, held on March 7. Applications also poured in for the Eva Fan Rally, the event held to celebrate the launch of the movie. 2,300 lucky winners were chosen from over 20,000 applicants, and even though all seats were allotted, it didn't stop fans from lining up outside the event from 9.00 in the morning.

The event included a talk show with Eva voice actors, a concert and a cosplay competition. One cosplayer claimed to have spent over 200 hours creating her costume - a wearable replica of Eva-01. The release of Death and Rebirth was described as a social phenomenon, and anyone who hadn't heard of the anime before, certainly knew about it now. Nothing like it has been seen since, and the popularity of Evangelion continues to surprise even the most jaded anime fan.

What is the relationship between Adam, Lilith and Lilim? 38

Adam and Lilith are two separate entities. However, as Ryoji Kaji doesn't once use the term Lilith, we can surmise that he is unable to understand the difference between the two.

However, as we learn from the Misato, "We too, us human beings, are the 18th Angel, and like Adam we were born from Lilith." Adam and Lilith therefore are two separate entities, but both the source of life.

According to one oral tradition, in the story of Creation, Lilith was the estranged wife of Adam. Even though the Angels put the fear of God in her, she would not change her mind, and refused to return to her husband. She later married Lucifer and gave birth to Lilim - a demon.

According to a different legend, Lilith was none other than the serpent that beguiled Eve into eating the Fruit of Knowledge. God in his anger removed her legs, leaving her to crawl on her stomach for the rest of her life.

Another story handed down through the

See Glossary
Adam
Lilith
Ryoji Kaji
Misato Katsuragi
Angel
Lilim
Fruit of Knowledge

ages is that Lilith was the goddess of the moon - a demoness - leading a gang of lunar monsters.

However, no matter which oral tradition we refer to, there is no suggestion that Adam and Lilith are one and the same entity. Unlike Eve, Lilith was not born of Adam, nor did Lilith give birth to Adam.

From the different legends we can conclude that Lilith is cursed, and becomes either a serpent, the wife of Lucifer or the goddess of the moon. Her association with Lucifer produces the child Lilim- a demon.

From the words of both Kaoru - "You Lilim" - and Misato - "Human beings, like Adam, were born of a life-form called Lilith." - we are able to establish one simple equation: Being the descendants of Lilith and Lucifer, human beings are all demons.

In Episode 17 Gendo says, "Mankind chased from the Garden of Eden and forced to escape to Earth to live cheek and jowl with death. The knowledge he acquired was the result of being the weakest of all creations..." Gendo says this to explain the state of humans when they were in the paradise deep within the bowels of Earth - the Egg of Lilith - before they were cursed with Original Sin, and before they produced the AT Field.

And when Fuyutsuki remarks, "Some ten

See Glossary
Kaoru Nagisa
Gendo Ikari
Egg of Lilith
AT Field
Kozo Fuyutsuki

years from now, the Third Impact will occur here," he is implying that GeoFront is in fact the Egg of Lilith.

Based on the sad realization that humans are demons, we can draw the following conclusions as illustrated by the following lines.

SEELE: "Man has forgotten his previous folly, and will repeat his mistakes."
SEELE: "If man does not repent, he will not change."
SEELE: "This is a rite-of-passage. So man who is closed off can be revitalized."
SEELE: "The destiny of destruction is also the joy of rebirth."
SEELE: "God, man and all living things will eventually become one through death."
Gendo Ikari: "No, that's wrong. We do not revert to nothingness. Everything merely reverts to the beginning."
Gendo Ikari: "We merely revert to the mother-figure, which has been lost to this world."
Gendo Ikari: "All hearts become one and gain eternal repose. No more than that."

It is ironic that Gendo's comments effectively explain the workings of the SEELE Human Completion Plan, and not his own.

The process of repenting, of returning to the mother's egg - Lilith - and the reversion of all living things to the beginning is basically the path followed by the SEELE Human Completion Plan. Except that this time around mankind will be born not as the offspring of Lucifer, but as the child of Adam recognized by God.

See Glossary
Third Impact
GeoFront
SEELE
Human Completion Plan

See questions
6 7 10 11
33 34 35 36
37 39 40 41
42 43 44

EVA File 003

The Tie-in Explosion

The release in October 1995 of Neon Genesis Evangelion on Japanese TV ignited a boom in merchandise unprecedented in a country already awash with such goods. As if overnight, well over 600 different items were made to commemorate the event. Figures were the most popular, with the inimitable bandaged Rei outselling all else. The Eva girls, kitted out in swimwear and striking suggestive poses, were, overall, a huge success, and things went a bit too far. One company offered a full-size 160-cm- (5.25") high Rei Ayanami for an unsettling $2,700. The full-size price tag didn't prevent the limited edition of 30 selling out immediately, young men making up the majority of the punters.

Evangelion goods soon invaded the game center. At a dollar a pop, the crane game was ideally suited to fans of robot anime. Figures, of course, were there to be had, but more appealing were the Evangelion bed sheets, which depicted a full-size Rei or Asuka asleep. Other Eva household items that ended up at the game center were bath towels and soap dishes. In fact, the latter, with figures of Rei, Asuka or Misato affixed, proved so popular that a second edition was released.

Figures kept on coming: Rei in Chinese dress, Asuka in sportswear, Misato in bikini, and Ritsuko in Santa Claus outfit. Eva fans knew that they were onto a good thing. The figures were overly detailed and well-made for game center-giveaways, and those in the know did their best to keep the news from spreading.

What actually are the Evangelions? 39

In the Bible, Eve is born of Adam. In terms of Evangelion, this is underscored by Kaoru, who says to Eva-02, "Alter-ego of Adam, servant of Lilith. Eve is made of the same flesh and blood as myself. For I too was born of Adam."

At the same time that Ryoji Kaji transports Eva-02 from Germany, he also brings the Bakelite Adam with him. From this, we can be almost certain that Eva-02 was created from Adam in Germany.

However, Eva-00 and the Eva-01 were completed before Adam was brought to NERV.

In Episode 21 Gendo tells Fuyutsuki, "This is the Eva-00, the model for our Adam Regeneration Plan, known as the E-Plan." Why is it a model? Is it because Eva-00 is not an official Eva created from Adam, but one created from Lilith?

The Eva-02 was designed in Japan but completed in Germany. The only reason we can give as to why it was completed in Germany is

See Glossary
Adam
Evangelion
Kaoru Nagisa
Lilith
Ryoji Kaji
Bakelite
NERV
Gendo Ikari
Kozo Fuyutsuki
Adam Regeneration Plan
E-Plan

that Adam was also in Germany at the time. When Asuka comes to Japan she notes that Eva-02 is "the first Evangelion in the world developed for real fighting."

In Episode 25, developed from the movie version, Keel Lorentz sees that Eva-00 has been destroyed and pins his hopes on Eva-01 saying, "Let's hope Eva-01, the only alter-ego of Lilith, can fulfill the mission."

There is also a scene where Kaoru says, "The Eva series is a curse on humans born of Adam. I just cannot understand why the Lilim have chosen to use this thing in an attempt to continue living."

What bothers Kaoru is that it is not possible for the Lilim, born of Lucifer and the very Lilith who fled Adam's side, to maintain good relations with Eve, born of, and then married to, Adam.

When Kaoru discovers the entity in Central Dogma is Lilith, he nods in understanding, "Wait, that's Lilith! So, that's what you Lilim are all about." Kaoru finally realizes human beings are not attempting to use Eve, born of Adam, as a way of living on, but are using the very mother of mankind - Lilith - as a way to regenerate themselves.

See Glossary
Asuka Langley Soryu
Keel Lorentz
Central Dogma
Lilim

What does the stabbing of Adam with the Spear of Longinus signify? 40

It is first important to explain what the Spear of Longinus is. Legend has it that Spear of Longinus is a weapon through which the world can be controlled, and which will bestow the holder with power.

However, the original Spear of Longinus was the spear used to stab Christ while crucified on the cross. The legends gifting the spear with sacred powers emerged after it was believed that the Roman soldier who owned it miraculously recovered from a chronic ailment. The story goes that he was cured by the blood of Christ that fell onto the spear. There are also stories of people inflicted with lifelong diseases or of bleeding to death after being stabbed with the spear.

Although tales of the Spear of Longinus are inevitably tied to blood, the overriding quality of the spear is that it is endowed with the powers of both death and rebirth.

There is one other important point that should not be overlooked: the Spear of Longinus

See Glossary
Spear of Longinus

was brought back from Antarctica and used to stab Lilith while she slept in the depths of Central Dogma. This stabbing is carried out by Rei, and after the spear is withdrawn Lilith's belly expands.

So, what does the stabbing of Adam with the Spear of Longinus signify?

When the giant Adam is stabbed with the spear, which controls both life and death, the AT Field is penetrated and human DNA fuses with the giant. This means that the spear is smeared with the blood of Adam, which contains both human and Angel elements.

The same spear is now used to stab Lilith. This then means the blood of Adam mixes with that of Lilith, who conceives as a result. The blood in this instance should be viewed as DNA, symbolized by the spiral of helix pattern carved by the spear as it flies through the air.

There is one further role for the Spear of Longinus, and that is of course to deal the *coup de grace* to the sacrifice crucified on the Tree of Life in order to atone for the sins of mankind.

See Glossary
Antarctica
Lilith
Central Dogma
Rei Ayanami
Adam
AT Field
Angel
Tree of Life

See questions
21 33 34 35
36 37 38 39
41 42 43 44

What actually happened at the Second Impact? 41

One of the major problems in answering this question is that a large part of the testimony about the Second Impact is contradictory. Let's try going over it.

1. Episode 20, Scene of the Second Impact

"Stop the surface light emission! It's breaking the threshold!"

"The DNA transplanted in Adam has also completed physical fusion"

"The AT Field is wide open"

This is the scene where the scientists are transplanting human DNA into Adam.

2. Episode 25, Intelligence acquired by Misato

"The Second Impact that took place 15 years ago was set off by human beings. But they did manage to keep the damage down to a minimum by having Adam revert to the egg before the other Angels awoke."

See Glossary
Adam
Misato Katsuragi
AT Field
Angel
Second Impact

We discover from Misato that the aim of the Second Impact was to return Adam to the egg. We can only get to the truth of the Second Impact by sifting through the contradictions.

Let's take a look as some other evidence relating to the Second Impact.

3. Episode 21, Fuyutsuki

"We have identified the area, the changes in the atmospheric components, and the total disappearance of all life-forms right down to microorganisms. There is a gigantic void close to the bombsite, and then there's that Giant of Light. This case is full of mysteries."

We know from this that the Second Impact is no simple explosion.

4. Episode 26, Maya Ibuki

"All the signs closely resemble what happened 15 years ago. So, are these warnings of a Third Impact then?"

This does indeed point to the Third Impact. And from that we realize that the Second and Third Impacts are phenomena that closely resemble each other. One of the things that Maya is pointing to is the anti-AT Field generated by the mass-produced Evas.

See Glossary
Kozo Fuyutsuki
Giant of Light
Maya Ibuki
Third Impact
Anti-AT Field
Evangelion

On the other hand, when Maya says, "All the signs," if indeed "All the signs," were equal at any given point, we would have to assume that both the phenomena immediately preceding and immediately following those signs would also have to closely resemble each other. And from that we can assume that the course followed by the Second and Third Impacts are very similar.

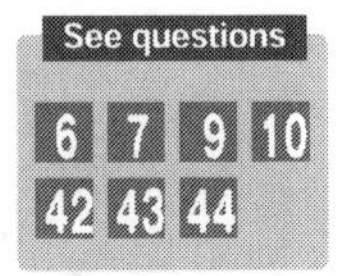

The problem is how to make this testimony consistent.

EVA File 004

Eva Goes to Hollywood

News of the coming live action Evangelion movie was first announced at the 2003 Cannes Film Festival. Details appearing on American conceptual art Web sites soon after revealed that production would be a joint effort between Gainax, ADV Films and Wata Workshop.

The involvement of Academy Award-winning Wata Workshop, a New Zealand-based special effects studio best known for its work on Lord of the Rings, already has Evangelion fans predicting an Eva-dominated Oscars in the not-too-distant future.

The film is still in early production and few details are available. But if the concept art is anything to go by, Rei Ayanami's seat is reserved at the Kodak Theater.

Eva characters have long been popular with Japanese cosplayers. But with the announcement of a live-action movie remake, American cosplayers have finally seen the light.

How do the Second and Third Impacts closely resemble each other? 42

Let's first quickly run through the major points of the Third Impact.

1. Eva-01 acquires the capabilities of the Fruit of Knowledge and the Tree of Life.
2. The Spear of Longinus pierces the core of Eva-01.
3. An anti-AT Field is generated.
4. Hall of Gaffe opened.
5. The AT Field recedes, the bodies of humans melt into LCL, while their souls revert to the Gaffe - the Egg of Lilith.

Based on this, let's now go back and review the Second Impact.

1. Eva-01 acquires the capabilities of the Fruit of Knowledge and the Fruit of Life.

At the Second Impact there were also circumstances closely resembling those outlined in Episode 26 when Fuyutsuki says, "We have acquired both the Fruit of Life held by the

See Glossary
Third Impact
Evangelion
Fruit of Knowledge
Tree of Life
Spear of Longinus
Core
Anti-AT Field
Hall of Gaffe
AT Field
LCL
Egg of Lilith
Second Impact
Fruit of Life
Kozo Fuyutsuki

Angels and the Fruit of Knowledge held by humans."

As can be seen from, "The DNA transplanted into Adam has also completed physical fusion," it is clear that Adam had fused with humans before the Second Impact. In other words, the Fruit of Life and the Fruit of Knowledge combined to become one before both the Second and the Third Impacts, giving birth to a life-form with powers equal to those of God.

2.The Spear of Longinus pierces the core of Eva-01.

At the Third Impact a spear that flies from the moon pierces the core of Eva-01. As can be seen from such lines as, "The spear, recover the spear," although it is clear that the Spear of Longinus was used at the Second Impact as well, it is uncertain how it was used.

But, if the Second and the Third Impacts are as similar as suggested, we can assume that the Spear of Longinus was used to pierce Adam at the Second Impact.

3. Anti-AT Field is generated.

The Third Impact elicits such lines as, "The anti-AT Field emerging from Lilith is expanding even further! It's materialized." And, "The anti-AT

See Glossary
Angel
Adam
Lilith

Field has broken through the critical point."

Similar lines from the Second Impact include, "The AT-Field has been totally removed." We can see from both of these lines that there was an expansion in the anti-AT Field.

4. Hall of Gaffe opened

At the Third Impact Fuyutsuki says, "The Hall of Gaffe has opened. Is this the opening of the door to the beginning and the end of the world?" At the Second Impact too, there is the line, "Commence the heat-extinguishing process as soon as the Doors of Gaffe open."

5. The AT Field recedes, the bodies of the humans melt into LCL, while their souls revert to the Gaffe - the Egg of Lilith

At the Third Impact, while humans melt away and become LCL, their souls return to the Black Moon - the Egg of Lilith. Keel says, "The end and the beginning are in the same place. Yes, this is how it should be."

The Second Impact has the following situation: in Episode 25 Misato says, "The Second Impact that took place 15 years ago was set off by human beings. But they did manage to keep the damage down to a minimum by having Adam revert to the egg before the other Angels awoke."

See Glossary
Black Moon
Keel Lorentz
Misato Katsuragi

In place of the Egg of Lilith - the Black Moon - we find out that there is a White Moon in Antarctica, or the Egg of Adam. The original meaning of the Second Impact was to have Adam's soul revert to the White Moon, as that of the Third Impact was to have the souls of human beings revert to the Black Moon - or Egg of Lilith.

So we can arrange the various testimonies as follows:

Third Impact
Eva, which holds the Fruit of Knowledge and the Fruit of Life
The Spear of Longinus pierces the core of the Eva
Expansion of the anti-AT Field
Opening of the Hall of Gaffe
Humans revert to the Egg of Lilith, the Black Moon

Second Impact
Adam fuses with human DNA
Adam is pierced with the Spear of Longinus
Expansion of the anti-AT Field
Opening of the Hall of Gaffe
Adam reverts to the egg, the White Moon

See Glossary
Antarctica

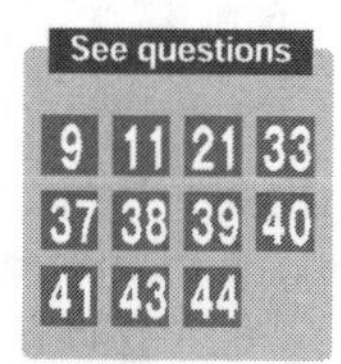

What were the scientists trying to do at the Second Impact? 43

In Episode 25 Misato says, "The Second Impact that took place 15 years ago was set off by human beings. But they did manage to keep the damage down to a minimum by having Adam revert to the egg before the other Angels awoke."

However, for Adam to revert to the egg requires the anti-AT Field, which is the power of God. And to gain those powers, it is necessary to fuse the Fruit of Life with the Fruit of Knowledge, in other words Angels and humans. That can be seen in Episode 26 when Fuyutsuki says, "We have acquired both the Fruit of Life held by the Angels and the Fruit of Knowledge held by humans."

And that is why human DNA was transplanted into Adam, as illustrated from the lines, "The DNA transplanted into Adam has also completed physical fusion." In order for fusion to take place it was also necessary to penetrate the AT Field with the Spear of Longinus, and if we assume that a similar set of circumstances as

See Glossary
Second Impact
Misato Katsuragi
Adam
Angel
Anti-AT Field
Fruit of Life
Fruit of Knowledge
Kozo Fuyutsuki
AT Field
Spear of Longinus

those at the Third Impact arose, then we can also assume that the core was pierced.

Adam generates the anti-AT Field so that the Spear of Longinus can acquire the Freudian death wish, and that sees the human DNA successfully transplanted into Adam.

At this stage, Adam acquires the Fruit of Knowledge and the Fruit of Life, and takes on the powers of God. As a result, Adam begins to generate the power of God in the form of an overwhelmingly powerful anti-AT Field from his entire body, becoming the Giant of Light. As can be seen by such lines as, "Stop the surface light emission! It's breaking the threshold," the scientists fear that all life-forms will be destroyed, reverting to LCL

This powerful anti-AT Field sucks all life within a specified distance into it and reverts it to LCL.

As can be seen from Fuyutsuki's lines in Episode 21, a number of phenomena occur that cannot be explained by the explosion alone. What he says is, "We have identified the area, the changes in the atmospheric components, and the total disappearance of all life-forms right down to micro-organisms. There is a gigantic void close to the bomb-site, and then there's that Giant of Light. This case is full of mysteries."

It is likely that the scientists mostly

See Glossary
Third Impact
Core
Giant of Light
LCL

believed they were carrying out a DNA fusion experiment. But senior SEELE officials should have been able to foresee that Adam would emit an excessive anti-AT Field once he had acquired the Fruit of Knowledge and the Fruit of life.

That's especially so when we remember their original intention was to see Adam revert to the egg. So that's probably why they took the precaution of wiring everything with explosives so they could escape immediately before anything happened.

While the scientists may have been able to foresee the results of the DNA fusion using the anti-AT Field, they had no prior knowledge of what would happen when the Fruit of Knowledge fused with the Fruit of Life.

That we know from the following conversation:

Keel: "Scientists have a tendency to believe in themselves too much."
Gendo: "Does that strike you as hypocritical then?"
Keel: "They have too many illusions. Those guys just don't have a tight enough grip on reality."
Gendo: "And it's those guys who are seeking the truth. Kind of ironic, eh?"

See Glossary
SEELE
Keel Lorentz
Gendo Ikari

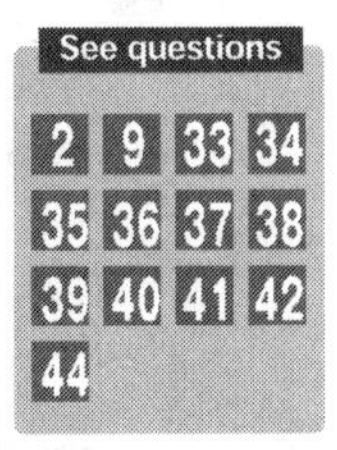

EVA File 005

Eva Merchandise '97: $300 Million

In the year Death and Rebirth was released, estimated sales of Evangelion merchandise topped $300 million. 70 percent of this was from sales of video and laser disks (2.26 million copies), three soundtrack CDs (910,000 copies), three theme song single CDs (880,000 copies), four-disk set CD-ROM (200,000 copies) and the three-volume manga (3.5 million copies). The soundtrack reached No. 1 on the album charts, the first for an anime since Adieu Galaxy Express 999 some 17 years before. Furthermore, over 600 Eva items, such as figures and toys, telephone cards and stationery, were released, pushing sales well over $300 million for 1997 alone! To estimate total Eva merchandise sales to date is a near-impossible task.

Top Eva Merchandise Sales (in number of items) in 1997

Video and laser disks	2.26 million
Soundtrack CD	910,000
CD single	880,000
CD-ROM	200,000
Manga	3.5 million
Movie book	3 million

What is the Hall of Gaffe? 44

The Hall of Gaffe that appears at the end of the tale and in the movie version originally comes from Jewish mythology, and is the room where the souls of children still to be born reside.

At the beginning of *Death and Rebirth*, we enter upon a scene under the Antarctic base in the year 2000, which reads "UN Underground Base 02." This tells us that one of the two underground bases under the control of the UN is in Antarctica. Needless to say, the other is in GeoFront in Japan.

Also, from the lines, "All workers below the second level evacuate at once to the upper sections of Central Dogma," we know that this is also called Central Dogma. Meanwhile, from the lines, "We have to treat the Spear of Longinus before it goes underground," we find out that there are even deeper underground locations, that there is a giant there, and that he will be pierced with the Spear of Longinus.

From what we have just seen we can

See Glossary
Hall of Gaffe
Antarctica
GeoFront
Central Dogma
Spear of Longinus

confirm that the underground base in the Antarctic has the same structure as that in Japan.

We also discover that Lilith is crucified in the depths of Central Dogma in Japan and has been pierced by the Spear of Longinus, in much the same way that Adam is crucified below the South Pole, and pierced by the Spear of Longinus by the Katsuragi expedition setting off the Second Impact.

We can confirm that both these underground bases are in fact the Hall of Gaffe. We only have to refer to;

SEELE: "Let's return GeoFront to its original form."
Fuyutsuki: "I don't see how after all this, human beings can desire to revert to the Egg of Lilith, the source of all life."
Fuyutsuki: "The portal to the Hall of Gaffe is opening. So, the door to the beginning and the end of the world is opening, is it?"

Lines related to the GeoFront in Antarctica:
"Commence heat-extinguishing process at the same time as the portal of the Hall of Gaffe opens."

So, how are these two different?

See Glossary
Lilith
Adam
Katsuragi Expedition
Second Impact
SEELE
Kozo Fuyutsuki
Egg of Lilith

In Japan we have, "The Egg of Lilith, the source of all life." It is from here that the soul of mankind is born and returns.

As opposed to this, in Antarctica, while there is no specific, "Egg of Adam," when Misato says, "They did manage to keep the damage down to a minimum by having Adam revert to the egg before the other Angels awoke," we can understand that this is the source from which the Angels are born and return.

The Katsuragi expedition carried out experiments with a number of objects in mind, and at the time of the Second Impact they open the portal to the Hall of Gaffe and conduct a heat-extinguishing process. As a result, any Angels born are instantly destroyed.

What that means in concrete terms is that Kaoru Nagisa, born on the day of the Second Impact, is the last of the Angels with roots in Adam, and no more are born. And that is what Misato means when she says, "They did manage to keep the damage down to a minimum, by having Adam revert to the egg before the other Angels awoke."

So, at last we find out the meaning of Ritsuko's words when she says, "The Hall of Gaffe was empty." The human Hall of Gaffe was not empty. That we know from the fact

See Glossary
Misato Katsuragi
Angel
Kaoru Nagisa
Ritsuko Akagi

that the children born in the year of the Second Impact, such as Shinji and Toji, exist.

However, despite this, Ritsuko says, "We have endowed the Evas, which originally had no soul at all, with a human soul." And, "This has all been salvaged, hasn't it?" Also, "She was the only girl who had a soul." As well as, "The Hall of Gaffe was empty. " And finally, "None of the Rei clones you see here have souls."

From this we can surmise the following: That it was necessary to include a human soul in the Evas, as the Hall of Gaffe was already empty when attempts were made to create the Evas, meaning they could not use Angel souls.

In the case of Rei, the intent was to use Angel souls all along, and despite the fact that the human Hall of Gaffe was not empty, there was no intention of including a human soul. This was impossible to achieve, however, because the Angel Hall of Gaffe was already empty. The Rei clones ended up as mere empty shells with no souls at all.

From all this we can see that there were in fact two Halls of Gaffe serving as the source of souls, and that one of these was the Egg of Lilith intended for human souls and stored in GeoFront in Japan.

See Glossary
Shinji Ikari
Toji Suzuhara
Evangelion
salvage
Rei Ayanami

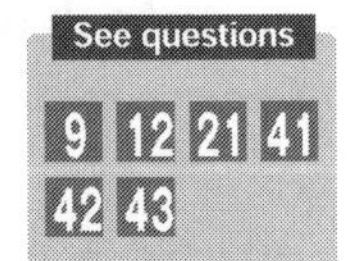

Why does Shinji strangle Asuka? 45

The scene of Shinji strangling Asuka attracted a flood of speculation when the movie was released, leading to endless debate as to why Shinji would do such a thing.

Aside from Old Testament quotes, there are numerous cases in Evangelion of far-reaching references to such Freudian concepts as the Libido and death wish.

To shed light on the cause of Shinji's sudden action, it is necessary to go over the psychological backdrop, extrapolated from the words and actions in Episode 25 - based on the movie version - and Episode 26.

Shinji: "I'm sick of everything. I just want to die. I don't want to do a thing."
Misato: "What are you whining about?"
Misato: "Get up! You're still alive."
Misato: "Give life everything you've got, then die."
Misato: "From here on, you're on your own.

See Glossary
Shinji Ikari
Asuka Langley Soryu
Libido
Misato Katsuragi

Decide everything by yourself. There is nobody out there to help you."
Shinji: "I can't do it. There's just no way I can do it. I have no right to kill and maim just to pilot the Evas. I thought there was nothing else but to become an Eva pilot, but I was just kidding myself. There's no value in someone as ignorant as me piloting the Evas. There's nothing I can do to help people. What I did to Asuka was terrible. I killed Kaoru too. There is not an ounce of kindness within me. I am a sly coward. I can do nothing but harm human beings. So, it's better for me to do nothing at all.

From this we can see that despite the kick in the pants from Misato, Shinji has lost his will to live.

Aoba: "Release the Evangelion series, S2 organ."
Hyuga: "The dimensional measurement has reversed itself. It is now showing a minus. It's become impossible to measure. It cannot be quantified.
Fuyutsuki: "Is that the anti-AT Field?"
Ibuki: "All phenomena now closely resemble the situation 15 years ago. So, is this a sign of the Third Impact?"

See Glossary
Evangelion
Kaoru Nagisa
Shigeru Aoba
S2 organ
Makoto Hyuga
Kozo Fuyutsuki
Anti-AT Field
Maya Ibuki
Third Impact

Self-Defense Forces: "S2 organ reaching critical levels. Abort the mission. All units to pull out immediately. We can no longer maintain inter-molecular gravity."

The generation of the anti-AT Field, and the failure to maintain inter-molecular gravity are both due to the death wish - the urge to die, destroy and the reversion to a primitive state.

SEELE: "Let's use the incomplete ego of the pilot from Eva-01 in the Human Completion Plan."
Aoba: "Psychological graph, signal down."
Hyuga: "Death drive dematerializing."
Fuyutsuki: "Can't the pilot's ego hold up any further?"
Shinji: "No! Stop!"
Kaoru: "So, you've had enough have you?"
Shinji: "So, that's where you were Kaoru?"
Aoba: "Solenoid graph reversing, ego limits weakening."
Fuyutsuki: "We have obtained both the Fruit of Life held by Angels and the Fruit of Knowledge from humans."
Fuyutsuki: "And we are now causing to revert to the Tree of Life, the embryo of life. The question is whether we can conjure an ark to save

See Glossary
Strategic Self-Defense Forces
SEELE
Pilot
Human Completion Plan
Fruit of Life
Angel
Fruit of Knowledge
Tree of Life

humans from the nothingness of the Third Impact. Or whether we are going to conjure up a demon to destroy mankind. The future is in the hands of Ikari's son."

By obtaining both the Fruit of Life and the Fruit of Knowledge Shinji acquires powers equal to those of God. The future is clearly in his hands. The problem is whether the world will return to nothingness thanks to Shinji's death wish. Ever since Kaoru was killed by Shinji, SEELE has attempted to destroy Shinji's ego, and use his death wish to send both himself and the world back to a primitive state.

Going off on a tangent, the choice of theme songs, "Thanatos - If I can't be yours" and "Come Sweet" both illustrate the importance of the death wish to the movie.

Yui: "Rei, you here and now are your own heart, and your own desire."
Rei: "What shall we wish for?"

The story so far has Shinji's ego weakening as a result of his death wish. From here on we get into Shinji's mental state, his inner space. What is it that Shinji wants?

See Glossary
Yui Ikari
Rei Ayanami

Shinji's Inner Space

Let's take a look at a scene that illustrates Shinji's mental state.

A: Kindergarten - Shinji makes pyramids in the sandpit with a little girl, but the girl's mother takes her home, leaving Shinji to complete the pyramid alone. He then destroys it and starts again.

B:Asuka, with an angry face, talking while seated on a bed.Asuka says, "Mama."

C: From the word "Mama" Shinji conjures up an image of Misato. Misato and Ryoji Kaji in bed with each other.
Misato: "So, I wasn't able to become Shinji's second mother."

D:The struggle between Asuka and Shinji.They kiss. Shinji licks his lips while looking at Asuka. Uncomprehending.
Asuka: "Just do it like you always do it. I'll just stand here watching you. If you cannot become mine completely, then I don't want anything."
Shinji: "So, you have to be kind to me."
Shinji ill at ease.

See Glossary
Ryoji Kaji

Shinji: "Don't reject me. Don't kill me."
Asuka: "Stop!"
Shinji strangles Asuka. His eyes warped with cruel joy.

E: Pictures painted by many children. A little boy with a spear and a little girl. The dead bodies of fish and a dog.

The first thing we pick up on from this peek into the inner world of Shinji is the cruel will to destroy. The destruction of the pyramid in A, Asuka's face in B, the verbal violence in D, then the pleasure Shinji derives from killing Asuka, along with the dead bodies of the fish and dog in E. These are all illustrations of Shinji's internal death wish, manifest in his desire for death and the wish for destruction.

Another issue that comes to the fore from such scenes as the bed scene with Asuka in B and with Misato in C, the kiss in D (followed by Shinji licking his lips) is the powerful sexuality. This illustrates Shinji's libido, the desire for sex and life.

The word "Mama" and the connection with the mother-figure that is the central image for A through C attests to the mother-child relationship being the starting point for both the libido and the death wish.

In other words, Shinji is caught up in a struggle of sex and death - the libido and the death wish. This calls forth numerous images from Shinji's memory, which he subtly alters and presents in the format we have just seen. In the final analysis, because this is a struggle between sex and death, it is death that inevitably wins.

Shinji: "You betrayed me. Betrayed my feelings."
Rei: "You misunderstood right from the very start. It was nothing more than a one-sided affair."
Shinji: "Nobody needs me. They can all go and die."
Shinji: "It's just the same to everyone whether I'm here or not. Nothing's gonna change. So, they can all go and die."
Rei: "Then what's your heart for?"
Shinji: "It would be better if it wasn't there at all. So, I'm gonna die."

Once we get to this point, we see Shinji's death wish has turned on him. Rei attempts to redirect Shinji's flow of thought, but Shinji doesn't listen. He desires only his own death.

Rei: "So, why are you here?"

Shinji: "Is it OK to be here?"
Silence
Shinji screams.

This is the first time that Shinji has shown any direct reaction to Rei's words, but now Rei herself is unable to come up with a worthy reply. This is similar to the scene when they are involved in the salvage operation, and Rei tells Shinji, "Decide for yourself." Shinji gets washed away on the wave of his death wish, and screams in the absence of anything worthwhile to say.

Hyuga: "The pilot's reaction is slipping closer and closer to zero."
Aoba: "The anti-AT Field generated by Lilith is expanding even further. It has materialized."
Hyuga: "The anti-AT Field has broken through the critical-point."
Aoba: "It's no good. At this rate we will not be able to hold the format of individual life-forms."
Fuyutsuki: "The doors of the Hall of Gaffe are opening. So, the door to the beginning and the end of life has opened, then?
Ibuki: "The AT Field...everyone's AT Field is disappearing."
Keel: "The beginning and the end are at the

See Glossary
Salvage
Lilith
Hall of Gaffe
AT Field
Keel Lorentz

same point. Right.This is the way it should be."

The death wish is also the urge to return to the origin. Shinji's ego is destroyed by this death drive, and in line with his desire to revert to nothingness, Lilith's anti-AT Field expands and everything reverts to the origin.

As a result, the material components of our bodies also revert to a kind of primordial soup, and our souls return to the Hall of Gaffe, where they resided before each of us were born.

The Libido

Let's look at some of the scenes that underscore Shinji's libido.

Shinji: "Ayanami, where the hell are we?"
Rei: "This is the LCL Sea. The primordial sea of life."
Rei: "It's a world where the AT Field has disappeared, and where we lose our very selves. A mixed up, ambiguous kind of place where none of us can tell where we end and others begin. A fragile world where we are everywhere, but nowhere."
Shinji: "Does that mean I'm dead?"
Rei: "No. It means everything has become as one."
Rei: "This is it! This is the very world you wanted."
Shinji: "But...this isn't it."
Shinji: "It doesn't feel right."
Rei: "If you once wish for the existence of human beings, then the walls of the heart will tear all humans apart"
Rei: "And that will set off another round of fear."
Shinji: "...enough."
Shinji: "Thank you."

See Glossary
LCL

This scene describes the generation of the AT Field after everything has become one through the death wish. This conversation suggests a sexual relationship between Shinji and Rei, indicating that the libido has been regenerated. As Rei is the mother of both Shinji and mankind, this also suggests sexual intercourse with the mother. This scene has much the same meaning as the breast-feeding scene in Episode 20.

From the fact that Shinji has carried Misato's crucifix about with him, we can see that it was Misato, who tried to become Shinji's mother, that spurred his desire to live as well as the events in Episode 20.

Rei: "If you can just conjure up the image of yourself, with your own strength, anybody can revert to a human form."
Yui: "No worries. All life forms have the strength to be reconstructed. If you just thank your lucky stars you are alive, then you can make a paradise out of wherever you're set down. After all, you're alive aren't you!"

It goes without saying that another way to express the powers of reconstruction maintained by all life forms, and their will to live, is the libido. All life forms encompass the death wish and the libido. So, while the world has reverted to its original state due to the death wish of Shinji, who has acquired powers rivaling those of God, reconstruction is possible via the powers of life - or the libido.

Let's now return to the original question and ask why does Shinji strangle Asuka.

Shinji strangles Asuka. Asuka strokes Shinji's cheek. Shinji weeps.
Asuka: "I don't feel too good."

Shinji, racked with guilt, then turns his death wish on himself, causing it to destroy his ego, distort the ego boundaries, fusing and reverting everything to its original state.

However, his libido works to generate an AT Field, and instead of a world where fears of others exist, Shinji opts for a world where he can be himself.

But what of the death wish that is present in all living things. The result of directing that death wish at oneself is the destruction of the ego. To avoid this happening the death wish is always directed at others. When Shinji is reconstructed after having his ego destroyed by his own death wish, he immediately directs that death wish at Asuka and strangles her.

This also reveals the real meaning of "others," taking on the idea that in order to preserve oneself, the death wish is inevitably directed at others. The true nature of the AT Field imposed between humans is that it is a zone of absolute fear.

We can see that we need others to act as the recipient of our death wish if we are to preserve ourselves as ourselves, and not have our ego destroyed by the death wish. In other words, humans cannot live alone. And that is the very meaning of the title of this last scene - "I need you."

Shinji - who has never loved anyone and never felt he loves himself either, who has tended to direct both his libido and his death wish at himself in the form of narcissism and self-punishment - weeps as he realizes all this only after his ego has been destroyed.

The libido and the death wish are closely tied; babies direct both at their "first other" - their mothers. Shinji, who has directed his death wish at Asuka, who accepts it, also targets her with his libido. This proves that he is capable of truly loving another. This is probably the real meaning of "Magokoro wo, Kimi ni - The End of Evangelion."

It is also worth adding that Asuka's "I

See questions
2 4 24 25
33 34 35 36
37 38 39 40
41 42 43 44

don't feel too good," is in answer to Shinji's call at the outset of the movie, "Asuka, Asuka, help, help, help, help, help," and the lines, "You're making fun of me as usual."

This has been a personal attempt to interpret the areas of Evangelion that many have found difficult to understand by using references to the Old Testament and Freudian psychology. These ideas are by no means those of the creators of the Evangelion series. There are just so many possible interpretations, which is why Evangelion has proved so popular.

Cosplay Model: Sono

Cosplay Model: Ran

EVA File 006

The Evangelion Revolution

Today Evangelion has a worldwide following. But, like so many great anime, its genius wasn't recognized when it was first broadcast in Japan. What helped generate Evangelion's popularity was the debate that evolved over the final two episodes, which left so many mysteries unresolved. The development of the Eva boom was therefore incomparable to anything that had come before. Below is a summary of how this boom unfolded.

1994 December: The comic serial begins in the manga digest Shonen Ace.

1995 October 4: The first episode of Neon Genesis Evangelion is broadcast on TV. Shinji's "I mustn't run away!" line becomes a catchphrase among hardcore fans.

November 22: Asuka's debut appearance in Episode 8. Her line "Are you an idiot?" becomes widely used among hardcore fans.

1996 January 31: Depiction of violence in Episode 18, in which the first Eva goes on a rampage and relentlessly pummels an Angel, is criticized as being unsuitable on an anime show that is viewed by children.

February 3: Genesis 0:1 video and LD, containing Episodes 1 and 2 of the televised anime, is released. Many fans are unable to buy it on the day of release due to a flood of preorders.

February 14: Broadcast of Episode 20 is criticized as inappropriate for children due to Misato's heavy breathing (although the love scene contains no explicit images).

March 27: Anime finale. Because the story's mysteries are left largely unsolved, the exchange of various opinions among fans heats up.

April 14: Director Hideaki Anno appears on radio and states that "anime fans need to have more self respect" and "come back to reality,"drawing criticism.

April 26: Gainax announces that it is creating an all-new Eva feature film. Simultaneously, it is announced that remakes of the final two episodes, along with all the televised episodes, will be released on video and LD.

May 10: Interview with director Hideaki Anno published in Newtype magazine. He comments that "Eva was created with an eye toward live action" and that "computer networking is graffiti on toilet walls," drawing more criticism.

May 22: The third volume of the television soundtrack CD, Neon Genesis Evangelion III, debuts at No. 1 on Oricon's album charts. The following day, even sports papers and variety shows report this as news.

June 2: Rei Ayanami selected for Mitaka City Bureau of Waterworks poster. There is a deluge of inquiries from fans, and a huge line forms from morning for an event in front of Mitaka Station to distribute note pads sporting the poster design. Commotion ensues as numbered tickets are hurriedly distributed.

July: In preparation for the all-new feature film, it is decided that a highlights collection from the 24 televised episodes and the new versions of the last two episodes will be shown in theaters in the spring of '97.

November 1: Production press conference for the movie Neon Genesis Evangelion: Death and Rebirth. It is revealed that the movie will introduce new Evas -05 through -13.

November 23: Advance tickets, which include an original telephone card, are released. Some people line up the night before, and lines exceed 2000 people.

December 8: Eva wins in the television division of the Kobe City sponsored "Animation Kobe" animation grand prix.

December 31: The movie theater Shinjuku Milano holds "Evangelion All Night". 14 of the televised episodes are selected for screening. 1200 fans attend.

1997 **March 15:** The movie Neon Genesis Evangelion: Death and Rebirth hits theaters. On the opening day there are 150,000 attendees.

Glossary
and
Keyword Index

Glossary

09 System
The popular name given to the activation system in Eva-01, based on its activation ratio of 0.000000001%.
17-18

A10 nerve
The nerve that plays one of the most important roles in connecting the Eva and the pilot. Also known as the pleasure nerve. This nerve is also said to be strongly connected with lofty thoughts and the affection exhibited between parents and children or between lovers. Unlike other nerves, it has no function to restrain the secretion of neuro-transmitters.

Absorber
The name of the NERV shock-absorbing system. Used when the outer shell of GeoFront is exposed following the great explosion of the Third Impact.

AC Recorder
An apparatus for storing internally stored data in the Eva that cannot then be externally detected.

Activation
To put the Eva into a controllable status. The activation sequence is as follows. (Activation preparations) Cooling water discharge>Stop signal plug discharge>Insert entry plug>(First Connection)>Insert LCL>Connect major power source all circuits> Major power source all circuits power transmission>Activate starter system>Operating voltage breaks through critical levels>(Second Connection)>Insert synapse, make connection>Send pulse>Connect A10 nerve>All circuits normal>Power transmitted to upper muscles of left and right arms>All clear for total nerve connection>(Third Connection)>Break through absolute boundary line>Open two-way circuit>Harmonics normal>(Calculating synchro-ratio)>(Prepare to launch)>Umbilical bridge moved>First Lock-bolt deactivated>First restraining device deactivated>Second restraining device deactivated>Safety switches 1 through 15 deactivated>Complete internal electrical charging>All clear with external electrical source code>Move to exit portal>Launch>Deactivate final safety switches>Lift off
23-24, 27-38

Activation Index
The minimum synchro-ratio needed to activate the Eva.

Adam
The first Angel, discovered in the form of the Giant of Light at the South Pole. Until revealed by Kaoru to be otherwise, it was thought that Adam was being kept deep in the

bowels of the earth at NERV HQ. But the true identity of the pale living thing crucified is Lilith, and the real Adam is an embryo reverted to an egg by human experiments.
27-38, 43-44, 45-46, 47-48, 49-50, 61-62, 73-74, 75-76, 79-81, 101-103, 109-111, 117-119, 123-125, 127-128, 129-130, 131-133, 135-138, 139-141, 143-146

Adam Regeneration Plan
Along with the E-Project and the Human Completion Plan, one of the projects run by NERV under the instigation of the Human Completion Project Committee. Aimed at resurrecting and revitalizing the first Angel, Adam.
23-24, 43-44, 47-48, 49-50, 109-111, 127-128

Akaki Tsuchi no Misogi - Red Earth Purification Ceremony
Carried out by members of SEELE when GeoFront reverts to the Black Moon. For Catholics, the red earth is suggestive of the origins of Adam, while a Japanese "misogi" is a purification or sanctification ceremony. Still, there is nothing in Evangelion that necessarily links the two.

Alpine Renault A310
Misato's favorite car. The body is blue. In Evangelion we get to see a right-hand drive electric car model and a left-hand drive gasoline driven model. The right-hand drive model is partially destroyed by the shock waves from the N2 mine used against the third Angel.

Angels
The enemy of mankind. Forming an autonomous ultra-weapon group, the Angels transcend the definition of living and non-living matter. The Angels are composed of a light-like substance, combining particles and waves, though 99.8% of the unique wave patterns are the same as those of human beings. They carry a red orb, called a core, which is common to all Angels, and cease to be active if the core is destroyed or is extinguished. Some 17 Angels appear in the SEELE scenario, which attack Central Dogma aiming for Adam/ Lilith.
17-18, 19-20, 21, 27-38, 41-42, 43-44, 45-46, 49-50, 61-62, 63-65, 67, 69, 71-72, 83-84, 85-86, 95-96, 101-103, 105-107, 109-111, 113-115, 117-119, 123-125, 129-130, 131-133, 135-138, 139-141, 143-146, 147-161

Antarctica
Following the Second Impact in the year 2000, the whole area melts becoming LCL; a world of death punctuated by pillars of salt. The appearance of this lifeless world has been compared to the Dead Sea. Because the earth has been thrown off its axis, temperatures rise by five to eight degrees, melting the ice. Because of an irregular magnetic field, there is a permanent aurora.
27-38, 45-46, 47-48, 51-52, 53, 71-72, 85-86, 129-130, 101-103, 135-138, 143-146

Anti-AT Field
The energy that neutralizes the AT Field, and which is generated by Lilith, who has assimilated with Rei. The energy materializes as a gigantic Rei-figure during the Third Impact. It expunges the AT Field - the walls of our hearts - in all humans, reverting them to a murky sea of LCL.
109-111, 131-133, 135-138, 139-141, 147-161

Apoptosis
Programmed cell-death aimed at biological control or self-defense. Necrosis is also a form of apoptosis, and is the opposite of mitosis.

Ariel
The 15th Angel.
27-38, 71-72

Armisael
The 16th Angel.
27-38

Asuka Langley Soryu
Second Children, and the pilot of Eva-02. She has Japanese and German blood. She graduated from a German university at the age of 14.
25-26, 47-48, 57-58, 83-84, 87-88, 95-96, 101-103, 113-115, 127-128, 147-161

AT Field
Short for Absolute Terror Field. Emits a topological space to neutralize physical attacks. According to Kaoru Nagisa, the AT Field is, "a sacred zone that cannot be violated by anyone, and the wall around our hearts that everyone has." It was originally thought that only Angels and Evas possessed AT Fields, but in actual fact, as Kaoru points out, it is a defensive wall that we all possess - the wall around our hearts that separates us from others.
19-20, 27-38, 41-42, 61-62, 113-115, 123-125, 129-130, 131-133, 135-138, 139-141, 147-161

AT-17
An important order issued by the Japanese Government for the live capture of the eighth Angel, as well as the freezing of all existing assets.

Bakelite
A form of heat-hardened resin. It has similar qualities to ultra-fast drying concrete. Bakelite was used in stopping Eva-00, which had veered out of control, and in the transportation of Adam.
117-119, 127-128

Bardiel
The 13th Angel.
27-38

Black Moon
The name given to the egg of Lilith, the source of life. With the activation of the Third Impact, it was discovered that GeoFront itself is the Black Moon.
113-115, 135-138

Central Dogma
The name of the underground facility, extending deep into the bowels

of the earth some seven kilometers below NERV HQ. This is where experiments on Eva-00 and Eva-01 were conducted. The lowest levels are known as Terminal Dogma.
27-38, 43-44, 47-48, 51-52, 71-72, 79-81, 87-88, 127-128, 129-130, 143-146

Children
The name given to children who have the ability to synch with the Evas. They are given the names First Children, Second Children, etc. depending on the order in which they were chosen for the task. Rei Ayanami represents the First Children, Asuka Langley Soryu the Second Children, Shinji Ikari the Third Children, Toji Suzuhara the Fourth Children and Kaoru Nagisa the Fifth Children. The use of the plural, when there is generally only one child per grouping, may be tied in with the use of the term "God's Children" in the New Testament.
25-26, 57-58

Colonies
The state formed by single units that choose to band together, even while maintaining the capacity to live independently. The Human Completion Plan as expounded by SEELE aimed at taking that defective colony called the human race, which had backed itself up against a wall with no further capacity for development, and have it evolve into a perfect single unit.
27-38

Comfort 17 Condominium
The name of the condominium where Misato lives, on the outskirts of New Tokyo-3. With 12 floors and 158 rooms, Misato lives at 11-A-2 on the 11th floor.

Core
The name of the red orb common to all Angels. The Angels cease to be active if the core is destroyed or is extinguished. The connection with the S2 organ remains unclear. It is also worth noting that although it is hidden by the restraining equipment, Eva-01 has a similar orb embedded in its chest.
17-18, 23-24, 25-26, 27-38, 47-48, 55, 79-81, 83-84, 135-138, 139-141

D17
The name of the special declaration issued by Misato with the authority invested in her by NERV during the attack by the 10th Angel. Transmitted to every ministry in the Japanese government, it is a directive for all civilians within a 50 km radius of ground zero to evacuate.

Destrude
The impulsive urge toward self-destruction as described by E. Weiss. Destrude is the opposite of the Libido.

Dr Katsuragi
Misato's father and the chief proponent of the S2 theory. He leads the expedition to investigate the Giant of Light, believed to be the first

Angel, Adam. A dyed-in-the-wool scientist; he was absent from his home and family for long periods, neglecting his wife and daughter. He takes the 14-year-old Misato with him on his trip to Antarctica, and sacrifices himself so she may survive the Second Impact.
85-86

Dummy System
The system designed to activate and control the Evas, even in the absence of a pilot, by performing pseudo-emulation of the thought patterns of the pilot and having the Evas recognize them as synchro-conditions. Unlike the dummy-plug, the system can be used as a back-up even when the pilot is present in the cockpit.

E-Incident
The name given to the battle between Eva-01 and the third Angel, Sachiel. As it was a battle in the city streets, there were many civilian casualties. Toji's younger sister sustained a serious wound in this incident.

E-Plan
The abbreviation of the Evangelion Project. Along with the Adam Project and the Human Completion Plan, one of the projects run by NERV under the instigation of the Human Completion Project Committee. Aimed at creating the Evas based on what has been discovered from investigations and research into Adam.
109-111, 127-128

Egg of Lilith
A gigantic sphere cited as the source of all life. Also known as the Black Moon. The Egg of Lilith is cited as having set off the First Impact, some four billion years ago, which turned an earth without life into a sea of LCL that gave birth to life.
105-107, 113-115, 123-125, 135-138, 143-146

Entry Plug
The cylindrical plug the pilot sits in when controlling the Eva. A kind of cockpit that is filled out with L.C.L. It is possible to control everything in the entry plug, apart from the weaponry, with thought control via the neural connectors in the interface-headset.
19-20, 27-38, 79-81, 113-115

Eva Electric Supply Outlet
A three-point outlet attached to the end of the umbilical cable in order to perform a connection with the Evas. Has two blast-bolts, which are used when connecting.

Eva Long-Distance Transportation Craft
A flying wing craft designed to transport the Evas. Uses eight large-scale rocket boosters to take off and land. The Eva is fixed by a lock-bolt to the lower portion of the central section of the craft, and released in mid-flight above its intended destination.

The craft has a capacity of ten people including the pilot.

Evangelion
The official name is "General Purpose Humanoid Battle Weapon Android Evangelion." The Evangelions were created within a mere 14 years, and at astronomical cost, as a means with which to oppose the Angels. The pilots are selected for their compatibility with the core of specific craft from among the Children, controlling the craft via neural connections beginning with the A 10 nerve.
17-18, 19-20, 21-22, 23-24, 25-26, 27-38, 41-42, 43-44, 45-46, 47-48, 55, 57-58, 61-62, 69, 75-76, 77-78, 79-81, 83-84, 85-86, 89-91, 93-94, 95-96, 97-98, 101-103, 105-107, 109-111, 113-115, 117-119, 127-128, 131-133, 135-138, 143-146, 147-161

Evangelion's Three Stooges
The name Asuka and Hikari give to the combination of Shinji, Toji and Kensuke.

External Electric Power Socket
The socket for connecting the umbilical cable to the back of the EVA.

F-type Equipment
Short for FLIGHT Equipment. Displays the status of equipment when the Eva is in flight. D-type and B-type equipment also exist.

First Impact
The first major catastrophe to visit the earth some four billion years ago. Said to have been caused by the impact of a massive meteorite hitting the earth, the First Impact was in fact due to the impact of the Egg of Lilith. That caused the portal to the Hall of Gaffe to open, allowing life to flood on to the face of the earth.
45-46

Fruit of Knowledge
An attribute of humans, who alone of all living things are endowed with this capability. In real terms we can consider it to be Science. As opposed to the Fruit of Knowledge, the Angels are endowed with the Fruit of Life.
101-103, 105-107, 109-111, 113-115, 123-125, 135-138, 139-141, 147-161

Fruit of Life
Represents the material attributes of the Angels, as opposed to the Fruit of Knowledge that is an aspect of human beings. In keeping with the book of Genesis, which says that those who eat of the Fruit of Life will enjoy eternal life, there is a close connection with the S2 organ, which is the perpetual organ of the Angels themselves.
101-103, 105-107, 109-111, 135-138, 139-141, 147-162

Gaghiel
The sixth Angel.
27-38

GEHIRN
The investigative arm of the Human

Completion Project Committee. GEHIRN was disbanded in 2010 when Noako Akagi completed the MAGI system, and all the project members, with the exception of Dr Akagi were transferred to NERV, the executive body of the overall plan.
117-119

Gendo Ikari
Supreme Commander of NERV and the father of Shinji. He is cool, calm and collected, and will do anything to achieve his goals. At the same time, he develops an unusual attachment for Rei and Eva-01. Forges ahead with the E-Project, the Adam Project and the Human Completion Plan all at once.
19-20, 23-24, 43-44, 47-48, 49-50, 61-62, 71-72, 79-81, 83-84, 87-88, 89-91, 93-94, 95-96, 101-103, 105-107, 109-111, 113-115, 117-119, 123-125, 127-128, 139-141

GeoFront
The mysterious and gigantic space constructed by NERV deep in the bowels of the earth below New Tokyo-3. A semi-circular space six kilometers in diameter and 0.9 kilometers high, 89% of which is now buried. The underground facility manages to maintain light at the same intensity as on the surface by channeling sunlight underground through optical fibers connected to light condensing blocks on the surface.
27-38, 43-44, 47-48, 49-50, 51-52, 71-72, 89-91, 123-125, 143-146

Giant of Light
Used to mean Adam, who appeared without warning in Antarctica in the year 2000. His silhouette is very close to that of the Evas, and he carries restraining tackle on his shoulders and something resembling a core in his chest. The Katsuragi expedition sets out to investigate, but runs into the Second Impact.
17-18, 27-38, 117-119, 131-133, 139-141

Hall of Gaffe
Meaning the door to both the beginning and the end of the world, and the hall of souls. When exposed to the power of the Hall of Gaffe all living forms lose their ability to maintain themselves as individual life-forms, reverting to LCL. At the Second Impact the door to the Hall of Gaffe is opened by Adam, and everything changes into a sea of LCL. At the Third Impact the portal is opened once again by Rei, who has assimilated with Lilith, and all life-forms revert to LCL.
135-138, 143-146, 147-161

Heaven's Door
The name of the entrance to the room where Lilith is held in Terminal Dogma.

Hikari Horaki
Prefect of class 2A at New Tokyo-3 Metropolitan Junior High School that Shinji attends.

Human Completion Plan
One of the major projects pursued by NERV under the jurisdiction of the Human Completion Project Committee, along with the Adam project and the E-project. The Human Completion Plan aims to compensate for the failures and shortcomings of humans, and produce a perfect human being. The problem is that SEELE and Gendo Ikari interpret this entirely differently. SEELE is looking to use the Evas to set off the Third Impact and have humans, who have run out of fresh initiative, surrender their individuality and evolve into a single amorphous, yet perfect, unit. Gendo, on the other hand, seeks to have human beings help each other in patching up the mental or emotional weaknesses that we all carry.
19-20, 23-24, 41-42, 43-44, 61-62, 63-65, 71-72, 89-91, 95-96, 109-111, 123-125, 147-161

Human Completion Project Committee
The name of the secret UN organization made up of members from Germany, UK, USA, Russia and France, and chaired by Keel Lorentz. The committee directs and oversees the NERV Human Completion Plan, based on the secret Dead Sea Scrolls held by SEELE.

Humans
The 18th Angel, born from Lilith, the source of all life. Kaoru refers to humans as Lilim. Humans possess the Fruit of Knowledge, as opposed to the Fruit of Life held by the other Angels.
101-103

Interface Headset
The interface the pilots wear on their heads to carry out neural connection with the Evas.

Ireul
The 11th Angel.
27-38

Israfel
The seventh Angel.
27-38

Jet Alone
The unmanned anti-Angel combat robot produced by the Japan Heavy Industrial and Chemical Corporation at the orders of the Japanese government. Known as JA, the robot is mounted with a mini-nuclear reactor, making it possible to achieve a maximum of 150 days of uninterrupted operations. But a sabotage operation by NERV intelligence sends the robot on an uncontrolled rampage at the unveiling ceremony in Old Tokyo, setting off the risk of meltdown. That was enough to see the plan sent back to the drawing board.
67, 69, 87-88

Kabbalah
Kabbalah is one part of Jewish mysticism. It consists of a large body of speculation on the nature of divinity, the creation, the origin and fate

of the soul, and the role of human beings that has been handed down over the centuries. The Tree of Sephiroth and the Tree of Life both appear in Kabbalism.
73-74, 117-119

Kaoru Nagisa
Fifth Children sent in by SEELE. He takes over as pilot of Eva-02 from Asuka, exhibiting an unusually high synchro-ratio. He turns out to be an Angel in human form.
27-38, 41-42, 47-48, 49-50, 57-58, 73-74, 109-111, 113-115, 117-119 123-125, 127-128, 143-146, 147-161

Katsuragi Expedition
The name of the expedition dispatched to investigate the Giant of Light, which had emerged in Antarctica. It is named after Misato's father who leads the expedition. Comprising mostly GEHIRN members, the expedition receives the backing of SEELE. It is this expedition that is hit by the Second Impact, which kills everyone except Misato.
143-146

Keel Lorentz
Lorentz is a German, he is chairman of the committee for the Human Completion Plan, and one of the 12 key members of SEELE. He is a mystery, something that is reinforced by the visor he always wears. He takes control of NERV after being betrayed by Gendo, and plans the Human Completion Plan using Eva-01. During the Third Impact it is discovered that every part of Lorentz from his backbone down is mechanized.
43-44, 71-72, 105-107, 127-128, 135-138, 139-141, 147-161

Kensuke Aida
A classmate of Shinji at the No.1 Junior High School in New Tokyo-3, Kensuke is an open kid with a friendly personality. He is into military goods and videos, and always walks around with a video camera. Shinji, Toji and Kensuke make up Evangelion's three stooges.
27-38

Kozo Fuyutsuki
Sub-commander of NERV. Fuyutsuki originally taught meta-biology at Kyoto University, but following the Second Impact was invited by Gendo to join NERV - or GEHIRN as it was still known at that stage.
23-24, 43-44, 71-72, 87-88, 89-91, 95-96, 101-103, 123-125, 127-128, 131-133, 135-138, 139-141, 143-146, 147-161

Kyoko Zeppelin Soryu
The mother of Asuka, who works in the German sub-branch of GEHIRN. She is mentally affected during the contact tests with Eva-02, suffering a severe psychiatric disorder as a result. From then on she lives in a dream world talking to a doll as though it were Asuka and ignoring her real daughter. She ends up committing suicide, but her soul lives on in the body of Eva-02.
25-26, 83-84, 113-115

LCL
Short for Link Connected Liquid. The transparent yellow liquid injected into the entry plug. Once the lungs are filled, it is possible to breath in the same way as in the atmosphere. The purple liquid in Antarctica and Central Dogma is also known as LCL.
19-20, 41-42, 79-81, 135-138, 139-141, 147-161

Leliel
The 12th Angel.
27-38

Libido
A psychic energy deemed in psychology to be at the base of all human endeavors. Freud termed this sexual instinct "sex drive," while Jung defined it as "life force," the source of all instinctive energy. The opposite of Destrude.
147-161

Lilim
The term that Kaoru uses when he refers to human beings. According to the Bible, Lilith was Adam's first wife, but she fled from his side, had an affair with Lucifer, and gave birth to the child, Lilim.
27-38, 49-50, 123-125, 127-128

Lilith
The giant crucified to the massive cross, and pierced through the breast by the Spear of Longinus, deep in Terminal Dogma below NERV. Until Kaoru saw that this was actually Lilith, everyone believed it to be Adam and called it so. In the Bible, Lilith was the first wife of Adam, but they had a falling out, as Lilith demanded the same rights as Adam. She later gave birth to the demon Lilim following her association with Lucifer.
27-38, 43-44, 47-48, 49-50, 61-62, 63-65, 109-111, 113-115, 123-125, 127-128, 129-130, 135-138, 143-146, 147-161

Lockbolt
The tool used to fix and hold the Evas. Used also with the umbilical bridge and the Eva long-distance transporter.

MAGI System
The super-computer composed of three independent blocks and mounted with a personality transfer operating system and controls the entire NERV system. The blocks are name Melchior, Balthasar, and Casper, each being endowed with a portion of the personality of the scientist, the personality of the mother, and the personality of Naoko Katsuragi, who developed the system. These three blocks create dilemma based on their different systems and decide the issue via majority decision. Computers with similar specs run not only in NERV, but also Germany, the US, China and Matsushiro.
27-38, 59-60, 93-94

Makoto Hyuga
Hyuga is in charge of intelligence at the military operations department of NERV.
147-161

Matriel
The ninth Angel.
27-38

Matsushiro
Location of the NERV lab. The lab was used frequently, but was destroyed by the 13th Angel during an activation test on EVA-03.
27-38

Maya Ibuki
Operator in the first section of the Technical Bureau at NERV. Ibuki is responsible for monitoring the Eva pilots.
131-133, 147-161

Misato Katsuragi
Head of military operations at NERV. The 29-year-old Misato is the life of the party, but is also a strong person at heart. Friends with Ryoji and Ritsuko at the No. 2 Tokyo University.
43-44, 51-52, 53, 85-86, 87-88, 95-96, 113-115, 123-125, 131-133, 135-138, 139-141, 143-146, 147-161

Mount Asama
The reactivated volcano where the eighth Angel, Sandalphon, is discovered in chrysalis form.
27-38, 95-96

Mount Asama Seismological Observation Post
The post from which Misato and Hyuga were dispatched after irregular activity was detected in the volcanic crater of Asama. They use an unmanned spotter craft to discover the Angel at a depth of 140 meters. Misato then orders special directive A-17.

Muldock Organization
An advisory organization involved in the selection of eligible candidates as Eva pilots, reporting directly to the Human Completion Project Committee. The organization exists in name only, and is nothing more than a front for NERV itself.
25-26, 55, 57-58

N2 bomb
The weapon with the most destructive power of any of the ordinance used by such fighting forces as the UN Force and the Strategic Self-Defense Forces. N2 is cited as being short for "No Nuclear," but the truth remains unclear. The N2 exhibited no effective destructive power against Angels with AT Fields, but still managed to destroy the special armor at GeoFront during the attack on NERV.
51-52

Naoko Akagi
Ritsuko's mother. An important member of GEHIRN, she developed the MAGI system. She has a love affair with Gendo, but when she

hears from Rei that Gendo is referring to her as, "An old woman past her sell-by date," she strangles Rei in a fit of rage. She then commits suicide by throwing herself into Casper.
59-60, 79-81, 93-94, 101-103, 117-119

NERV (Special Organ)
A special unit that comes directly under the UN, and is set up to investigate, research and destroy the Angels. Gendo Ikari is supreme commander and Kozo Fuyutsuki subcommander. The headquarters of NERV are in Japan, with sub-branches one and two in the US, subbranch three in Germany, and other branches spread throughout the world.
21, 23-24, 25-26, 27-38, 43-44, 45-46, 47-48, 51-52, 55, 59-60, 61-62, 69,71-72, 85-86, 87-88, 93-94, 95-96, 127-128

Neural Connection
The process by which two-way neural-communication and synchronicity is achieved between the pilot and the Evas, using LCL, the interface-headset and plug-suits. It is also possible to modify neural connection from the command post at NERV HQ.

New Tokyo-2
The new capital built in Matsumoto in Nagano following the destruction of Old Tokyo by the dropping of the new bomb during the military clash of September 20, 2000. The new capital was already up and running by the start of 2003, and adequately performing its function as a capital city after rapidly recovering from the Second Impact. Having said which, a decision on the second relocation of the state capital is taken in 2004, and the capital moves to near Lake Ashi.

New Tokyo-3
The city fortress built near Lake Ashi to repulse the Angels following the decision on the second relocation of the state capital taken in 2004. The city exists amid an array of armored buildings, including reserve weapon silos, electricity supply sources and the egress and recovery shoot for the Evas. The many tall buildings that dot the landscape are designed to be stored in GeoFront in event of an attack.
27-38, 43-44, 45-46, 51-52

New Tokyo-3 No. 1 Junior High School
The school Shinji attends. His class - 2A - gathers together the candidates for the Fourth Children.

Old Tokyo
Destroyed by the dropping of the new bomb during the military clash of September 20, 2000 immediately following the Second Impact. An emergency meeting of the provisional government decided to move the capital to Matsumoto city in Nagano.

Out of Control
What happens when the Eva operates outside of pilot control. Eva that go out of control are violent in nature, and exhibit overwhelmingly strong fighting capabilities. Eva-00 went out of control twice and Eva-01 three times. Eva-02 has never gone out of control, but this is likely to be connected with the fact that the soul of this Eva was withdrawn until the attack on NERV by the SSDF.
27-38

Pallet-rifle
A major Eva weapon, which fires depleted uranium shells at high speed.
27-38

PenPen
The name of the genetically modified Spring Penguin that Misato keeps as a pet. A male, PenPen loves hot baths, but sleeps in the freezer. He has sharp claws on the ends of his wings, which he opens and closes with a button on his shoulder. He constantly walks around carrying something white on his back, but what it is is not clear. PenPen clearly has a high IQ as he can understand and speak with humans, and read the newspaper. The number on his nameplate is BX293A.
53

Pillar of Salt
The white pillar-like formations that shoot up out of the LCL sea seen in Antarctica and Central Dogma. In the Old Testament, when Lot and his family are escaping from the conflagration visited upon Sodom and Gomorrah, they are told by God not to look back. But Lot's wife chooses to look back, despite what God has said, and is transformed into a pillar of salt.

Pilot
Used interchangeably with "Children," the pilot controls the Eva.
17-18, 19-20, 23-24, 25-26, 55, 57-58, 69, 77-78, 79-81, 83-84, 95-96, 113-115, 147-161

Plug Suit
Combat gear worn by the pilot when he enters the Eva. The suit fits the body like a glove and maintains life-support and neural connection support functions.
27-38

Positron Sniper Rifle
A revamped positron cannon specially designed for the Evas, NERV technical development department section 3 modified a prototype self-propelled positron cannon commandeered from the SSDF technological research facility. The firing system is based on positrons being generated from a circular-accelerator, aimed and fired. The positron rifle destroys the target by reacting to the component electrons of the target and generating pair-annihilation energy.

Progressive Knife
A high-oscillation particle knife. Developed for use by the Eva in close quarters fighting, it cuts all matter it comes into contact with at the molecular level. Known as a Progknife, it is normally stored in the parts of the left shoulder. Eva-02's Progknife is in the form of a retractable knife, so even if the tip is missing a replacement blade can be inserted.
17-18

Purge
The forced separation of the umbilical cable from the external electricity source socket. In the battle against the seventh Angel, purging is used to allow the Eva to attack at full throttle and top speed.

R-Alert
An emergency evacuation alert for D-level staff in NERV HQ

Ramiel
The fifth Angel.
27-38

Rei Ayanami
First Children and pilot assigned to Eva-00. Born in the No. 3 Lab at the Human Evolution Research Institute, the first Rei was murdered by Naoko Akagi and the second perished along with one of the Angels. The one we see here is third generation Rei.
19-20, 25-26, 27-38, 57-58, 71-72, 79-81, 83-84, 93-94, 97-98, 101-103, 105-107, 113-115, 129-130, 143-146, 147-161

Ritsuko Akagi
Systems Administrator and head of the Technology Department at NERV HQ. Ritsuko is responsible for the E-Project and is the effective No.3 at NERV, after Commander Ikari and second in command Fuyutsuki. She comes across as detached and intelligent, with something of the scientist's unworldliness. She has been friends with Misato since they were both at the No.2 Tokyo University.
47-48, 59-60, 79-81, 93-94, 95-96, 143-146

Ryoji Kaji
Head of the Special Surveillance department at NERV, an investigator for the Japanese government, and also a spy for SEELE - a triple agent. On the surface Ryoji seems a little on the light side, but also exhibits a philosophical approach to life. Ryoji has been friends with Misato and Ritsuko since they attended the No. 2 Tokyo University. He lived with Misato at university, and they get back together again after Ryoji is assigned to HQ from the German sub-branch.
27-38, 47-48, 49-50, 85-86, 87-88, 123-125, 127-128, 147-161

S2 Organ
Abbreviation of the "Super Solenoid Engine." Cited as the source of power for the Angels, as in the theory promoted by Dr Katsuragi. When

we consider that Eva-01 achieved unlimited operational time after importing the S2 engine of the 14th Angel, Zeruel, we can see that it is a type of perpetual engine. Also, as both the Angels with S2 engines and the mass-produced Eva have cores, we can surmise that the core and the S2 engine are inseparably linked.
21, 109-111, 147-161

S2 Theory
The abbreviation of the "Super Solenoid Theory." A theory of perpetual energy supply promoted by Dr Katsuragi. The theory was only at the hypothetical stage when promoted, but was unexpectedly provided with experimental underpinning by the emergence of an Angel endowed with a source of power explainable only by the S2 theory.

Sachiel
The third Angel.
27-38

Sahaquiel
The 10th Angel.
27-38

Salvage
The rescue of the pilot physically enclosed in the cockpit. Shinji, in the cockpit of Eva-01, was the object of salvage operations that failed. He was somehow able to escape from the cockpit despite the failed mission.
143-146, 147-161

Sandalphon
The eighth Angel.
27-38, 41-42

Second Impact
The biggest explosion since the dawn of history, which occurred at Mount Markham in Antarctica on September 13, 2000. Some two billion people lost their lives in the islands of the Southern hemisphere as the sea level rose as a result of a tidal wave and melting ice in the immediate aftermath of the explosion. The power of the explosion also knocked the earth off its axis, with the result that Japan now experiences perpetual summers. The official explanation of the explosion is that it was a natural disaster following the impact of a meteorite hitting the earth at close to the speed of light. But what really happened is that the explosion was set off artificially by SEELE and Gendo Ikari as they tried to make the first Angel revert to the egg - its DNA sample - before it awoke.
17-18, 25-26, 27-38, 45-46, 47-48, 51-52, 53, 85-86, 89-90, 101-103, 109-111, 117-119, 131-133, 135-138, 139-141, 143-146

Secret Dead Sea Scrolls
The text serving as the scenario, or the codename of the scenario, for the SEELE Human Completion Plan. The original Dead Sea Scrolls were discovered in a cave in Palestine in 1947, and are cited as having being left there by members of the

Qumran sect of Gnostics.
43-44, 63-65, 71-72, 89-91, 109-111

SEELE
The secret organization which controls NERV, through which it pursues the Human Completion Plan based on the readings of the secret Dead Sea Scrolls. As previously stated, the aim of the project is to see human beings surrender their individuality and evolve into a single amorphous, yet perfect, unit. The 12 component members of SEELE are represented as monolithic holograms.
23-24, 43-44, 49-50, 61-62, 63-65, 71-72, 87-88, 89-91, 95-96, 105-107, 109-111, 113-115, 123-125, 139-141, 143-146, 147-161

Shamshel
The fourth Angel.
27-38

Shigeru Aoba
In charge of communications at NERV Central Command. Longhaired, he enjoys playing the guitar. However, there is little explanation of his emotional make-up, and even in his final moments at the Third Impact, he is unable to conjure up the image of the person he loves.
147-161

Shinji Ikari
Third Children and the pilot assigned to Eva-01. Called up by NERV and forced to pilot Eva-01 against his own wishes. Develops some awareness as a pilot in the latter part of the story and begins to show a more positive side.
17-18, 23-24, 25-26, 51-52, 53, 55, 57-58, 77-78, 79-81, 83-84, 85-86, 95-96, 97-98, 101-103, 113-115, 143-146, 147-161

Shiro Tokita
Tokita belongs to Japan Heavy Industry and Chemical Engineering Corp., and is responsible for the development of Jet Alone. His sarcasm towards Ritsuko and Misato at the JA party is over the top, but when the JA goes out of control and threatens to go into nuclear meltdown, he hands Misato the password for the destruction of the entire program.

Sigma Unit
The name of a facility within Central Dogma. Split into such areas as D-17 with its No. 87 protein wall and D-18 with its No. 6 pipe. Contaminated by the 11th Angel, Ireul.

Spear of Longinus
A forked spear with a double-spiral that dovetails into a single point when thrown, and has the capability of piercing an AT Field. Discovered in the Dead Sea and carried to the Adam research facility in the South Pole. The spear is connected with the Second Impact, having being used in tests to activate Adam.
27-38, 49-50, 71-72, 101-103, 105-107, 109-111, 113-115, 117-119, 129-

130, 135-138, 139-141, 143-146

Strategic Self-Defense Forces (SSDF)
The organization set up in 2003 that reports directly to the Ministry of Defense. In the story of Evangelion, the Air, Land and Sea wings of Japan's Self-Defense Forces are incorporated into the UN Forces, but the SSDF remains under the control of the Japanese government.
147-161

Synchro-Ratio
The numerical reading that displays the synchronicity ratio between the Eva and the pilot when performing neural connection. The higher the reading, the greater the ability of the pilot to control the Eva at his will. It is apparently impossible to control the Eva with a reading of 10% or less.
25-26, 55, 69, 83-84

Tabris
The 17th Angel.
27-38

Terminal Dogma
The name of the zone at the lowest levels of Central Dogma. Aflood with a sea of LCL, pillars of salt abound in this area, which also features "Heaven's Door" behind which Lilith is crucified on the cross.

Third Impact
The third major disaster to be visited on the world following the First and Second Impacts. Cited as occurring through contact between the Angels and Adam, NERV aims to prevent this happening by repulsing the Angels. In the final analysis, the Third Impact is set off by the assimilation of Rei, who is pregnant with Adam, and Lilith, and the awakening of Eva-01. With the opening of the portal to the Hall of Gaffe all lifeforms on the face of the planet are no longer able to maintain themselves as independent units, reverting to an LCL sea.
19-20, 27-38, 43-44, 45-46, 61-62, 63-65, 71-72, 123-125, 131-133, 135-138, 139-141, 147-161

Toji Suzuhara
A classmate of Shinji in class A year 2 of the No. 3 New Tokyo Metropolitan Junior High School. He is a passionate individual whose feelings are expressed in an unadorned, no-nonsense manner. He focused his resentment on Shinji after his younger sister was injured in a battle between an Eva and an Angel, but has since made up, and they are now friends. Both his father and grandfather work in the research facility. Toji is chosen as the Fourth Children, and takes part in activation tests with Eva-03.
27-38, 57-58, 143-146

Tree of Life
A tree with roots in the heavens, and which spreads its branches to the earth. Also known as the Central Tree. Eva-01, which also absorbs the Spear of Longinus, transforms itself into this tree, which also represents

the River of Life.
73-74, 101-103, 105-107, 109-111, 113-115, 129-130, 135-138 147-161

Umbilical Bridge
The apparatus used to lock the craft when storing the Evas. It serves the purpose of a restraint, and is deactivated immediately before launching.

Umbilical Cable
The cable designed to provide an external electricity supply to the Evas. The umbilical cable connects to the back of the Eva via the electrical supply outlet. The cord serves a very important role for the Evas, which are able to run for only five minutes on their internal electricity supply alone.
21

Yashima Operation
The name of the operation to repulse the fifth Angel Ramiel. Employing a positron sniper rifle to fire on the target from long distance, the operation was named after "The Battle of Yashima," when Nasuno Yoichi hit a Japanese fan with his arrow from a considerable distance. Yashima is also one of the old names for Japan.

Yui Ikari
Mother of Shinji and wife of Gendo. Is absorbed by Eva-01 in 2004 during contact experiments. Believed to be an unforeseen incident at the time, the truth is it was a result of Yui's own will, as she accepted her fate of achieving eternal life and becoming the living proof of humanity.
23-24, 25-26, 79-81, 89-91, 95-96, 105-107, 113-115, 147-161

Zeruel
The 14th Angel.
21, 27-38

Keyword Index

E

F

G

H

T

U

W

Y

Z

From character goods to on-screen anime stars, the **MYSTERIES AND SECRETS REVEALED!** series brings you everything you never knew and more about your favorite anime and manga characters. Compiled in Tokyo, Japan, home of otaku culture, this series is unofficial and unrelenting in its quest to unearth the mysteries and secrets behind some of the world's most popular anime!

Coming soon in the MYSTERIES AND SECRETS REVEALED! series

The Lupin III File

Secret and Confidential

Since the '70s Lupin III has been a star of the anime screen. This amorous French master thief travels the world in search of easy riches and big rip-offs. **The Lupin III File** uncovers the secret life of this crafty cartoon hero. Who is he really? Why does he live the life he does? And what about the other characters that fill this action-comedy world? Everything you ever wanted to know about anime's most-loved crook can be found within the pages of this book.

$11.95 ISBN 0-9745961-7-5 July 2004

The Inu-yasha Experience

Fiction, Fantasy and Facts

In this mystical tale set in Japan's long-ago Era of the Warring States, Inu-yasha, the half-demon hero of the story, and Kagome, a Tokyo schoolgirl transported back in time, are thrown together in a quest to find the shattered pieces of the magical Shikon Jewel and return harmony to the world. **The Inu-yasha Experience** reveals the many secrets, subplots, character traits and behind-the-scenes gossip that have made this one of the most popular anime ever released on either side of the Pacific.

$11.95 ISBN 1-932897-08-9 August 2004

YuYu Hakusho

The Complete Guide

Since its manga launch in 1990, which sold 40 million copies in Japan, to the hit series on Cartoon Network, YuYu Hakusho has attracted anime fans of all stripes. The adventures of Yusuke, a tough teen delinquent who dies saving a child from a traffic accident and is reborn as a Spirit Detective, are played out in a fast-paced multi-dimensional world of supernatural baddies and doting teenage girls. **YuYu Hakusho: The Complete Guide** takes the reader on a whirlwind tour through Yusuke's many worlds, unearthing and explaining everything from story backgrounds and characters quirks to supernatural technologies and merchandise hot on the streets of Tokyo.

$11.95 ISBN 1-932897-09-7
October 2004

MYSTERIES AND SECRETS REVEALED! 1

The Gundam Explorer

Wing, First, G, SEED, and more!

Why does Char wear a mask?
Who or what is Shubertz Bruder?
What is Operation Meteor?
How does OMNI differ from the UESA?

Mobile Suit Gundam is recognized as the masterpiece of robot anime. The first TV show, which began in Japan in 1979, launched a series of feature animation that today still manages to wow even the most jaded mecha fan.

The Gundam Explorer reveals the mysteries and secrets of four televised Gundam sagas. From Wind, First and G to the newly-released SEED, this book guides the reader through a maze of character bios, Gundam technologies and truths and legends that continue to perplex and mesmerize fans all over the world.

$11.95 ISBN 0-9723124-8-X

MYSTERIES AND SECRETS REVEALED! 2

The Dragon Ball Z Legend

The Quest Continues

Who is the meanest DBZ dude?
What is a Scouter?
Why does Lunch disappear halfway through the series?
Which characters were added for the TV series?
When does Videl fall for Gohan?

In 1984, something remarkable happened in the world of Japanese manga. A boy with special powers met a girl with a dream, and together they set off to find seven magical balls. The boy's name was Goku, the girl's name Buruma, and the story, as we all know, is Dragon Ball.

The Dragon Ball Z Legend celebrates the 20th anniversary of Akira Toriyama's masterpiece with a fresh and fascinating tour through the most popular episodes of the long-running series. From the Tenkaichi Tournaments to the far-away Planet Namek, this book explores the fantastical worlds of Goku and the crazy cast of characters that have made Dragon Ball Z a global hit.

US$11.95 ISBN: 0-9723124-9-8